CHRISTMAS
COMFORT & JOY
Classic & Modern Recipes & Tips

Lovoni Walker
Jean Paré

Christmas Comfort & Joy

First Printing November 2012

Library and Archives Canada Cataloguing in Publication

Walker, Lovoni, 1965-
     Company's Coming Christmas comfort & joy / Lovoni Walker, Jean Paré.

(Special occasion series)

Includes index.

ISBN 978-1-927126-29-5

1. Christmas cooking. 2. Cookbooks. I. Paré, Jean, 1927-

II. Title. III. Title: Christmas comfort & joy.

IV. Title: Company's Coming Christmas comfort and joy.

V. Series: Special occasion series

TX739.2.C45W336 2012   641.5'686   C2012-901746-9

Portions of this book were previously published by Lone Pine Publishing as *The Essential Canadian Christmas Cookbook*, 2005. Recipes contributed by Jean Paré: Smoked Salmon-wrapped Scallops; Oven Wings; Grilled Brie and Fruit Crostini; Silky Butternut Squash Soup; Vegetable Quinoa Casserole; Wild Rice Medley; Freezer Almond Cranberry Buns; Figgy Orange Cake; Cream Cheese Tea Ring; Hint o' Mint Squares; Icebox Ribbons; Holiday Coffee and Tea.

Published by

Company's Coming Publishing Limited

2311 – 96 Street

Edmonton, Alberta, Canada T6N 1G3

Tel: 780-450-6223   Fax: 780-450-1857

www.companyscoming.com

Company's Coming is a registered trademark owned by Company's Coming Publishing Limited

We acknowledge the financial support of the Government of Canada through the Canada Book Fund for our publishing activities.

Printed in China

PC: 16

Contents

THE COMPANY'S COMING LEGACY

Jean Paré grew up with an understanding that family, friends and home cooking are the key ingredients for a good life. A busy mother of four, Jean developed a knack for creating quick and easy recipes using everyday ingredients. For 18 years, she operated a successful catering business from her home kitchen in the small prairie town of Vermilion, Alberta, Canada. During that time, she earned a reputation for great food, courteous service and reasonable prices. Steadily increasing demand for her recipes led to the founding of Company's Coming Publishing Limited in 1981.

The first Company's Coming cookbook, *150 Delicious Squares*, was an immediate bestseller. As more titles were introduced, the company quickly earned the distinction of publishing Canada's most popular cookbooks. Company's Coming continues to gain new supporters in Canada, the United States and throughout the world by adhering to Jean's Golden Rule of Cooking: Never share a recipe you wouldn't use yourself. It's an approach that has worked—millions of times over!

A familiar and trusted name in the kitchen, Company's Coming has extended its reach throughout the home with other types of books and products for everyday living.

Though humble about her achievements, Jean Paré is one of North America's most loved and recognized authors. The recipient of many awards, Jean was appointed Member of the Order of Canada, her country's highest lifetime achievement honour.

Today, Jean Paré's influence as founding author, mentor and moral compass is evident in all aspects of the company she founded. Every recipe created and every product produced upholds the family values and work ethic she instilled. Readers the world over will continue to be encouraged and inspired by her legacy for generations to come.

NUTRITION INFORMATION GUIDELINES

Each recipe is analyzed using the most current version of the Canadian Nutrient File from Health Canada, which is based on the United States Department of Agriculture (USDA) Nutrient Database.

- If more than one ingredient is listed (such as "butter or hard margarine"), or if a range is given (1 – 2 tsp., 5 – 10 mL), only the first ingredient or first amount is analyzed.
- For meat, poultry and fish, the serving size per person is based on the recommended 4 oz. (113 g) uncooked weight (without bone), which is 2 – 3 oz. (57 – 85 g) cooked weight (without bone)—approximately the size of a deck of playing cards.

- Milk used is 1% M.F. (milk fat), unless otherwise stated.
- Cooking oil used is canola oil, unless otherwise stated.
- Ingredients indicating "sprinkle," "optional," or "for garnish" are not included in the nutrition information.
- The fat in recipes and combination foods can vary greatly depending on the sources and types of fats used in each specific ingredient. For these reasons, the amount of saturated, monounsaturated and polyunsaturated fats may not add up to the total fat content.

INTRODUCTION

Cooking is such an integral part of our daily lives, no time more so than at Christmas. All the baking, roasting, chopping, mixing and love that goes into our holiday food is filled with tradition, but we also want to explore some different avenues and perhaps start some new traditions of our own.

Some of our most special memories focus on the food of the holiday season. A warm spice fragrance fills the air… butter and sugar are being creamed in the mixer… a new batch of cookies sits waiting to be baked while another sits cooling, ready to be decorated and transformed. Friends and family come around to share this special time of year, eagerly waiting to see what tempting morsels will be laid out for them.

Each year it seems the holiday season rolls around faster than the one before, and each year we all vow to be better organized this time—to have the shopping, the baking and the card writing all done in advance. Sometimes, though, the most well organized strategies don't happen as we plan.

During this busy time, it will be a comfort to have a cookbook filled with recipes for all your favourite foods to make for the holiday season. You don't have to go searching through pages of other cookbooks and magazines—from truffles and cookies for gifts to the perfect roasted turkey, the delicious recipes are all right here in one book.

At the end of most of the recipes you will find handy make-ahead tips, including freezing and reheating tips where appropriate. There are plenty of hints throughout to help you plan ahead for your festive season celebrations.

Of course we've included recipes for cooking the perfect Christmas Day meal, but we have also expanded beyond that day. We have recipes for appetizers for pre-Christmas parties or special meals you can have cooking in the oven while you are out hanging pretty lights, decorating the tree or playing in the snow… hearty, wholesome recipes to warm you and chase away the winter chills. Also included is a selection of party drinks and desserts that will tempt any soul.

Christmas is a time to reflect on who and what is important in our lives. It's a time to embrace the spirit that is Christmas and to cherish happy moments with family and friends. Make your festive cooking an enjoyable experience—cook with love, fill your house with delicious aromas, drink it all in and make this Christmas an extra special one.

May the Christmas season—and the recipes in this book—bring comfort and joy to all of you. Happy cooking!

In Our Kitchen

Here is some useful information about the ingredients, cooking terms and techniques we've used in this book. Cooking times provided are approximate and can vary according to different ovens and the type of cookware you use.

INGREDIENTS

Broth (stock) is bought prepared in a Tetra Pak or is homemade or, in a pinch, you can make it from bouillon powder mixed with water according to the directions on the package.

Butter is salted.

Citrus juices such as lemon, orange and lime are fresh.

Eggs are large.

Milk is 1%.

Mushrooms are small- to medium-sized, white or brown, unless otherwise specified.

Olive oil is extra-virgin unless otherwise specified.

Pepper is freshly ground for the best, most intense flavour.

Wines and sherry are alcoholic. Substitute chicken broth (in savoury recipes) if you prefer, but the flavour will differ from the original recipe.

MEASURING

Measure dry and semi-solid ingredients in dry-measure cups and level off using the straight edge of the back of a knife.

Measure liquids in glass or plastic liquid measures.

This book uses both imperial and metric measurements where appropriate. For items measured by weight, we have given the metric equivalent in grams. As most packaged dry goods indicate their weight in grams, our approach should make it easier for you to find and measure the correct quantity.

BAKING DISHES

To measure the capacity of a baking dish, fill it with water and then pour the water into a large measuring jug. The following measurement conversions are approximate and have been scaled either up or down.

4 cups/1 qt/1 L

6 cups/1 1/2 qt/1.5 L

8 cups/2 qt/2 L

10 cups/2 1/2 qt/2.5 L

12 cups/3 qt/3 L

BRUISING CARDAMOM PODS OR GARLIC

To bruise cardamom, place a pod on a cutting board and press down firmly using the flat side of a knife, the bottom of a saucepan or a meat mallet until the pod opens slightly.

To bruise garlic, place a clove on a cutting board and press down firmly using the flat side of a knife, the bottom of a saucepan or a meat mallet until the clove is slightly squashed.

HANDLING BEETS

Wear rubber gloves when handling beets to avoid staining your hands red.

HANDLING HOT PEPPERS

Hot peppers contain capsaicin in the seeds and ribs. Removing the seeds and ribs will reduce the heat of the peppers. Wear rubber gloves when handling hot peppers and avoid touching your eyes. Wash your hands well afterward.

HANDLING SQUASH

Some people have an allergic reaction to raw squash flesh, so wear rubber gloves when cutting or handling.

MAKING FRESH BREAD CRUMBS

To make fresh bread crumbs, place day-old bread in a food processor and process until fine (or coarse) crumbs. Bread crumbs can be stored in small freezer bags, sealed and placed in the freezer and thawed as needed.

MELTING CHOCOLATE

Method 1—Place chocolate in a small microwave-safe bowl. Do not cover. Microwave on 70% power in 40-second intervals until chocolate is almost melted. Stir until smooth and completely melted.

Method 2—Place chocolate in a medium heatproof bowl. Place bowl over small saucepan of simmering (not boiling) water, ensuring bowl is not sitting in water. Stir for 2 to 3 minutes until chocolate is almost melted. Remove bowl from heat and continue to stir until smooth and completely melted.

PIPING BAG

If you don't have a piping bag to use to pipe icings, use a freezer bag with the corner snipped off.

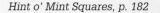

Hint o' Mint Squares, p. 182

Figgy Orange Cake, p. 138

TOASTING NUTS, SEEDS OR COCONUT

When toasting nuts, seeds or coconut, cooking times will vary for each type of nut—so toast them separately. For small amounts, place ingredient in an ungreased shallow frying pan. Heat on medium for 3 to 5 minutes, stirring often, until golden. For larger amounts, spread ingredient evenly in an ungreased shallow pan. Bake in a 350°F (175°C) oven for 5 to 10 minutes, stirring or shaking often, until golden.

USING YEAST

When using yeast, it is important for the liquid to be at the correct temperature. If the liquid is too cool, the yeast will not activate properly. If the liquid is too hot, the yeast will be destroyed. For best results, follow the recommended temperatures as instructed on the package.

ZEST AND JUICE

When a recipe calls for grated zest and juice (such as lemon juice and zest), it's easiest to grate the fruit first, then juice it. Be careful not to grate down to the pith (the white part of the peel), which is bitter and best avoided.

PARTY PLANNING TIPS

The days leading up to Christmas and through to New Year's Day are some of the busiest and most festive of the year. They're also when we tend to do more entertaining, and on a much larger scale, than other times of the year. And the holiday season would certainly not be complete without plenty of great food!

Sometimes, however, the holidays leave us tired and frazzled. You can help to avoid that by planning ahead and keeping your preparations as simple as possible. With these time-saving tips, you can host great get-togethers with plenty of fantastic food and still enjoy yourself!

Before planning any party or get-together, first consider your budget, your guest list and your type of event.

BUDGETING TIME AND MONEY

Consider your schedule and your budget. You don't want to plan parties so elaborate that you spend every waking moment coordinating them, or break the bank buying supplies. Set a budget that is realistic and feasible.

When budgeting, keep in mind the cost of food, beverages (both alcoholic and non-alcoholic) and any décor or special touches that you want to incorporate into your party. Choose seasonal fruits and vegetables that are more likely to be readily available and reasonably priced. Don't be afraid to purchase a few pre-made or convenience items that will help simplify your menu and save you some time.

YOUR GUEST LIST

When planning who to invite to your party, consider how many people will comfortably fit into your space. If you want to invite more people than you have room for, consider hosting a few smaller get-togethers. Smaller parties are often easier to organize, more casual and more intimate—which many guests prefer! If your party guests don't already know each other, think about who might mix and mingle well.

STYLE OF ENTERTAINING

Think about what type of party you'd like to have. You may have a particular theme or focus already in mind, such as an informal cookie exchange or a family Christmas Day feast, which will influence everything from the time of day you hold your get-together to the type of food served at it.

Most parties fall into one of three broad categories of serving styles: buffets, sit-down meals or cocktail parties.

Buffets

At a buffet, food is set out in large bowls or platters on a table or other serving area. Guests pick up their own plates and move past the food, serving themselves. Buffets work well for both small and large gatherings, and create a casual, relaxed atmosphere. Because your guests serve themselves, you have more time to mingle.

Buffets lend themselves well to potluck-style entertaining, where friends and family members each bring a dish. Another bonus of buffets is that they can easily be adapted for different courses and times of day—for example, you could host a dessert-only buffet at an evening party.

Sit-down Meals

Sit-down meals are more intimate. Guests are seated together at a table, allowing everyone to join in the conversation. Unless you have a very large space, sit-down meals are typically best suited for smaller gatherings—though the camaraderie and conversation they spark are appealing even when there are many gathered around the table.

Sit-down meals can be either formal or informal. For a formal affair, you can plate the food yourself and bring it out to your guests, course by course—like you'd expect at a restaurant. Since guests have little input at the time of service, you may wish to inquire about dietary preferences or restrictions in advance.

For more casual sit-down meals, pass bowls and platters from person to person at the table and let your guests serve themselves. Serving dishes are left on the table (space permitting) to allow for second helpings.

Cocktail Parties

Appetizers, snack-type foods, dips and canapés are the usual fare at cocktail parties, along with desserts. Because people move around and circulate at these type of parties, there's no need to set a table. However, you may wish to set up a few separate food and drink stations, along with several seating areas, to encourage mingling.

You can provide a wide variety of hors d'oeuvres in place of a full dinner at an evening gathering, or just a few dishes for guests to nibble on at an afternoon gathering. It can be as formal or informal as you like. And remember, at cocktail parties, the drinks are often just as important as the food.

Rum Balls, p. 170

MENU PLANNING

The next step in planning your gathering is setting your menu. If you're hosting a Christmas dinner, you may choose to go with a more traditional meal. Or, if you're hosting a potluck, you may want to request that guests bring a certain type of dish so that all bases are covered. Perhaps you don't wish to host a meal at all, but rather a cookie exchange or a dessert buffet. Or maybe you just want to have enough baking and goodies on hand so you can serve something sweet to guests who drop by for a quick visit.

It's important to consider how well the dishes you've selected can be prepared together. For example, with only one oven, you can't bake two dishes at two different temperatures at the same time. Try to select some items that can be made ahead and reheated, and some that can be assembled in a flash at the last minute.

To take some of the stress out of hosting, many recipes in this book can be made a few days ahead of time and chilled until ready to serve, or prepared and frozen a month or more in advance. Look for the Make-ahead Tips throughout the book that will help you get organized in advance.

Make a schedule of how long it will take to do everything and when it will all get done (and by who). When in doubt, overestimate the amount of time required. With a schedule in place, you'll know exactly when to cook the potatoes, and you won't forget about the hors d'oeuvres in the freezer that need to be thawed.

For any menu, don't forget to consider your guests' dietary restrictions. Be sure to also offer a few healthier options.

HOW MUCH FOOD?

Our recipes provide a good estimate of portion sizes, but when putting them together to create a meal or appetizer array, you may wish to consult the following handy list:

Type of Course	Amount Per Person
Appetizers	3 to 4 pieces if being served with a meal
	10 to 12 pieces for an appetizer-only party
Cheeses	1 to 2 oz. (28 to 57 g) if being served with a meal
	3 to 4 oz. (85 to 113 g) for an appetizer-only party
Salads	1 cup (250 mL) leafy greens
Meat	3 to 5 oz. (85 to 140 g) cooked weight
Fish & Shellfish	5 oz. (140 g) cooked weight
Pasta, Rice or Potatoes	1/2 to 1 cup (125 to 250 mL)
Vegetables	1/2 cup (125 mL) of each vegetable dish
Dessert	1/8 of a 9 inch (23 cm) pie or cake
Squares	3 to 4 pieces

Type of Beverage	Standard Serving Size
Beer	12 oz. (341 mL)
Wine or Champagne	5 oz. (142 mL)
Spirits	1 1/2 oz. (45 mL)

For every 26 oz. (750 mL) bottle of spirits, provide approximately 3 similarly sized bottles of mix. Also include three to five 6 oz. (170 mL) non-alcoholic drinks (such as punch) per guest. Plan for two to three cups of coffee or tea per guest.

Herb Butter Turkey p. 64

PREPARING YOUR HOME

Part of a good party is the setting. A few small adjustments can make a big difference.

Make sure there's room in your entryway for people to take off their coats and boots. Provide somewhere for guests to sit, if possible, and lay out an additional mat for boots. You may want to clear out a front closet or designate a room for storing coats.

Will people need to move between and within rooms? Perhaps you can rearrange furniture so people can move through the space more easily. Is there adequate seating? If you'll be setting up food and beverage tables, consider spacing them out to encourage mingling and avoid congestion.

Tidy your bathrooms. Provide enough hand towels. Stock extra toilet paper and tissues, and make sure the supply is easy for guests to see. A votive candle is a simple but elegant final touch.

DECORATING

The Christmas season is the one time of year when many people go all out with the holiday décor. There are colourful lights adorning the neighbourhood houses, a wreath on the door, a decorated tree in the living room, pine boughs around the staircase, Christmas cards and photos of loved ones displayed… Holiday decorations often feature prominently in our childhood memories and create a feeling of holiday magic.

But you don't have to go to extremes to create a festive atmosphere for your holiday get-together. Simple, small touches here and there go a long way.

The dinner or serving table is one place that deserves a special touch. If you have good china and silverware (or can borrow them from a lovely great aunt), this is the time to use them! But if not, don't fret—you can entertain very attractively by mixing and matching different colours, patterns, shapes and styles of plates, serving dishes and glassware. Consider how you can use what you already have on hand before purchasing (or borrowing) any new pieces.

For a sit-down meal, set your table in advance (that way, it will look like everything's under control even if you feel it isn't). To avoid cluttering up your table, remember that dessert plates, extra cutlery, and coffee and tea cups can brought out when needed rather than set out at the beginning of a meal.

A tablecloth or napkins can instantly add colour and a festive feel to a dining room or to any table. You could experiment with double layers in complementary (or monochromatic) colours, runners or varying overhang lengths.

Small decorative elements, such as sprigs of holly berries and greenery, can be an attractive touch. If you'd like a centrepiece for your dining room table or to dress up a dessert or beverage table, consider candles or a small vase of red, green and gold ribbons. When you're decorating, your goal is to create an inviting, approachable space. If you decide something looks overcrowded, simplify. Final touches shouldn't overpower your table or overshadow your food.

CLEANING UP

A little planning before your party makes cleaning up after it less of a chore.

- Use foil-lined pans or foil containers, for less mess and a quicker wash up.

- Wash, dry and put away as many preparation dishes as you can before the party.

- Empty your dishwasher and garbage can before the party.

- Make room in your refrigerator for leftovers.

- Have extra dishcloths handy for spills and splashes.

- Let others help!

Icebox Ribbons, p. 184

MINI SHRIMP ROLLS

Makes 15; serves 6 to 8

You can substitute lobster or crab for the shrimp if you prefer.

1 Tbsp (15 mL) butter

3 Tbsp (45 mL) dry sherry

1 lb (454 g) uncooked
medium shrimp
(peeled and deveined)

1/3 cup (75 mL) finely
chopped celery

1/3 cup (75 mL) finely
chopped green onion

2 Tbsp (30 mL) mayonnaise

1 Tbsp (15 mL) lemon juice

1/4 tsp (1 mL) salt

15 dinner rolls

cayenne pepper,
for sprinkling

Melt butter in a large frying pan on medium. Add sherry and heat until bubbling. Add shrimp and cook for about 2 minutes until pink and just cooked; do not overcook. Chop shrimp and place in medium bowl; cool.

Add next 5 ingredients and stir until well combined.

(continued on next page)

Cut dinner rolls across the top and almost through to bottom, taking care not to cut through. Spoon filling into each roll. Sprinkle with cayenne pepper.

1 roll: *180 Calories; 4.5 g Total Fat (1 g Mono, 1 g Poly, 1.5 g Sat); 50 mg Cholesterol; 22 g Carbohydrate; 1 g Fibre; 10 g Protein; 310 mg Sodium*

Make-ahead Tip

The filling can be made a day ahead; store in a sealed container in the refrigerator.

SHRIMP COCKTAIL WITH AVOCADO SAUCE

Serves 4

Take a step back in time with a revamped version of an old favourite—a simple, fun and delicious way to start a meal. Make the avocado sauce just before serving.

SHRIMP COCKTAIL

11 oz (310 g) bag large uncooked shrimp
(unpeeled)

1/2 tsp (2 mL) salt

AVOCADO SAUCE

1 large ripe avocado, halved and seed removed

2 Tbsp (30 mL) sour cream

1 1/2 Tbsp (25 mL) lime juice

1 Tbsp (15 mL) Thai sweet chili sauce

1/4 tsp (1 mL) salt

1 cup (250 mL) shredded romaine lettuce

Shrimp Cocktail: Place shrimp in a large steamer in a large saucepan over simmering water; sprinkle with salt. Steam for 2 to 3 minutes until pink and just cooked; do not overcook. Cool. Peel and devein shrimp, leaving tails intact.

Avocado Sauce: Mash avocado in a small bowl until smooth. Add next 4 ingredients and mix well.

Place a little shredded lettuce into bottom of 4 cocktail glasses. Arrange shrimp around edge of glasses. Place a spoonful of avocado sauce in centre of glasses.

1 serving: 180 Calories; 10 g Total Fat (5 g Mono, 1.5 g Poly, 2 g Sat); 120 mg Cholesterol; 8 g Carbohydrate; 4 g Fibre; 17 g Protein; 590 mg Sodium

Make-ahead Tip

The shrimp can be cooked and peeled 1 day ahead; store in a sealed container in the refrigerator.

SEAFOOD POUCHES WITH LIME DIPPING SAUCE

Makes about 60; serves 8 to 10

These tasty little morsels can either be deep-fried or steamed in a large bamboo steamer; we made the recipe in a two-tiered steamer. Steamers are available from Asian grocery stores. Serve hot.

SEAFOOD POUCHES

1 Tbsp (15 mL) canola oil

1/4 cup (60 mL) grated carrot

1/4 cup (60 mL) thinly sliced green onion

2 garlic cloves, minced

1 tsp (5 mL) finely grated ginger root

11 oz (310 g) bag scallops

11 oz (310 g) bag uncooked shrimp (peeled and deveined), finely chopped

2 Tbsp (30 mL) finely chopped fresh cilantro

1 1/2 Tbsp (25 mL) soy sauce

1 Tbsp (15 mL) Thai sweet chili sauce

1 lb (454 g) package round Shanghai dumpling wrappers (about 60), thawed if frozen

canola oil, for deep-frying

LIME DIPPING SAUCE

1/4 cup (60 mL) lime juice

3 Tbsp (45 mL) Thai sweet chili sauce

2 tsp (10 mL) soy sauce

1 tsp (5 mL) fish sauce

1 tsp (5 mL) sesame oil

Seafood Pouches: Combine first 5 ingredients in a small frying pan on medium-high. Cook for about 2 minutes until fragrant; spoon into a medium bowl.

Add next 5 ingredients, and stir until well combined.

Spoon a rounded teaspoon of mixture into centre of each dumpling wrapper. Lightly brush a little water around edge of wrapper. Bring wrapper up around filling and press to seal. Keep covered with tea towel to prevent drying out. Repeat with remaining filling and wrappers.

Deep-fried Variation: Heat oil to 350°F (175°C). Deep-fry pouches, in batches, for about 2 minutes until golden brown and cooked through; drain on paper towel.

Steamed Variation: Place half of pouches in a single layer in a large, greased bamboo steamer basket. Ensure pouches are not touching each other. Place steamer basket over large pot or Dutch oven of boiling water. Steamer should fit snugly into the top of the pot so very little steam escapes. Cover tightly and cook for about 15 minutes until wrappers are tender and seafood is cooked. Repeat with remaining pouches.

Lime Dipping Sauce: Combine all 5 ingredients in a small bowl. Serve pouches with lime dipping sauce.

1 seafood pouch with 1/2 tsp (2 mL) dipping sauce: 40 Calories; 1 g Total Fat (0 g Mono, 0 g Poly, 0 g Sat); 15 mg Cholesterol; 5 g Carbohydrate; 0 g Fibre; 3 g Protein; 115 mg Sodium

Make-ahead Tip
The seafood pouches can be made a day ahead. Store in refrigerator on parchment paper–lined baking sheets and cover with plastic wrap. Or you can freeze them and then transfer frozen pouches to a sealed container or sealable plastic bags for up to 1 month. Thaw, covered, in a single layer on parchment paper–lined baking sheets before cooking.

Smoked Salmon-wrapped Scallops

Makes 12; serves 6

Tender, juicy scallops wrapped in smoked salmon and grilled to perfection.

**24 thin slices of smoked salmon
(about 1/2 lb., 225 g)**

24 fresh (or frozen, thawed) large sea scallops, patted dry

**12 wooden 8 inch (20 cm) skewers,
soaked in water for 10 minutes**

3 Tbsp (45 mL) white wine vinegar

2 Tbsp (30 mL) basil pesto

2 tsp (10 mL) granulated sugar

Wrap 1 piece of salmon around each scallop. Thread 2 wrapped scallops, from edge to edge through diameter, onto each skewer.

Combine vinegar, pesto and sugar in a small bowl. Brush onto scallops. Preheat gas barbecue to medium (see Note). Cook scallops on greased grill for about 2 minutes per side, brushing with pesto mixture, until scallops are opaque. Discard any remaining mixture. Serve warm or cold.

*1 skewer: 70 Calories; 2.5 g Total Fat (0 g Mono, 0 g Poly, 0 g Sat);
20 mg Cholesterol; 2 g Carbohydrate; 0 g Fibre; 10 g Protein;
230 mg Sodium*

Note: If you don't want to barbecue, preheat broiler and broil the pesto-brushed scallop skewers on a greased baking sheet for 2 minutes on each side until opaque in the middle.

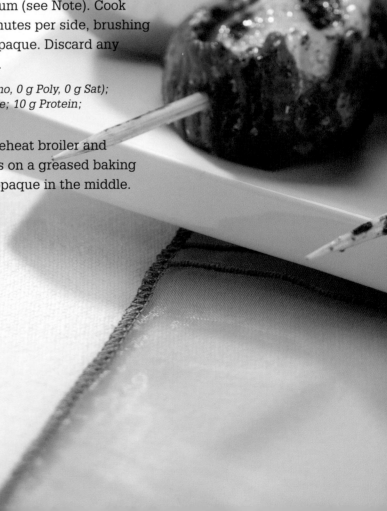

Sweet Chili Chicken Skewers with Lime Aioli

Makes 40; serves 8 to 10

These skewers are equally delicious served with Thai sweet chili sauce for dipping if you don't want to make the lime aioli.

SWEET CHILI CHICKEN

1/4 cup (60 mL) lime juice

1/4 cup (60 mL) Thai sweet chili sauce

3 Tbsp (45 mL) chopped fresh cilantro

3 Tbsp (45 mL) olive oil

1 Tbsp (15 mL) soy sauce

1/4 tsp (1 mL) pepper

5 boneless, skinless chicken breasts halves (4 – 6 oz, 113 – 170 g, each)

40 wooden 8 inch (20 cm) skewers, soaked in water for 10 minutes

olive oil, for brushing

LIME AIOLI

2 egg yolks (large)

3 garlic cloves, minced

2 Tbsp (30 mL) lime juice

pinch of salt

1 cup (250 mL) olive oil

2 Tbsp (30 mL) Thai sweet chili sauce

Sweet Chili Chicken: Combine first 6 ingredients in a large bowl.

Cut each chicken breast diagonally crosswise into thin slices. Add to marinade and toss to coat. Cover and refrigerate for 3 hours.

Remove chicken from marinade; discard marinade. Thread 1 piece of chicken lengthwise onto each skewer. Heat grill pan (such as cast-iron grill, barbecue or electric grill) on medium-high. Brush with olive oil. Cook chicken in 2 to 3 batches for about 3 minutes per side until fully cooked. Remove and cover with foil to keep warm while cooking remaining skewers.

Lime Aioli: Process first 4 ingredients in a food processor until well combined. With motor running, drizzle olive oil through feed chute in thin steady stream until thick. Add sweet chili sauce and process until well combined. Serve chicken with lime aioli.

1 skewer with 1 1/2 tsp (7 mL) lime aioli: 80 Calories; 6 g Total Fat (4.5 g Mono, 0.5 g Poly, 1 g Sat); 20 mg Cholesterol; 1 g Carbohydrate; 0 g Fibre; 3 g Protein; 40 mg Sodium

Make-ahead Tip

The lime aioli can be made 3 days ahead; store in a sealed container in the refrigerator. The marinade can be made 3 days ahead; store in a sealed container in the refrigerator.

OVEN WINGS

Makes about 36; serves 6 to 8

Remove skin or leave as is. Either way, the colour is dark and rich.

3 lbs (1.4 kg) chicken drumettes (or whole chicken wings)

1 cup (250 mL) chopped onion

1 green pepper, chopped

1 red pepper, chopped

3/4 cup (175 mL) soy sauce

3/4 cup (175 mL) water

1/3 cup (75 mL) brown sugar, packed

1/2 tsp (2 mL) seasoning salt

Preheat oven to 350°F (175°C). Arrange drumettes on a foil-lined baking sheet with sides. If using whole wings, discard wing tips and cut wings apart at joint.

Stir remaining 7 ingredients together in a medium bowl. Bake, uncovered, for about 1 hour until tender. Remove with slotted spoon or tongs to platter.

1 drumette: 100 Calories; 6 g Total Fat (0 g Mono, 0 g Poly, 1.5 g Sat); 30 mg Cholesterol; 3 g Carbohydrate; 0 g Fibre; 8 g Protein; 360 mg Sodium

Make-ahead Tip
Wings can be made 1 month ahead. Freeze in a sealable container and reheat to serve.

ALMOND MEATBALLS WITH YOGURT DIPPING SAUCE

Makes about 45 meatballs; serves 6

The meatballs can also be deep-fried in hot oil (350°F, 175°C) until browned and cooked through.

ALMOND MEATBALLS

1 Tbsp (15 mL) olive oil

1/2 cup (125 mL) finely chopped onion

2 garlic cloves, minced

1 tsp (5 mL) ground cumin

1/2 tsp (2 mL) pepper

1/4 tsp (1 mL) ground cinnamon

1 lb (454 g) lean ground beef

1/2 cup (125 mL) fine dry bread crumbs

1 large egg, fork-beaten

1/3 cup (75 mL) slivered almonds, toasted (see p. 8) and finely chopped

1/4 cup (60 mL) chopped fresh parsley

1/4 cup (60 mL) dried currants

1 tsp (5 mL) finely grated orange zest

YOGURT DIPPING SAUCE

3/4 cup (175 mL) plain yogurt

1 Tbsp (15 mL) lemon juice

1 Tbsp (15 mL) liquid honey

pinch of salt

1/4 tsp (1 mL) coarsely ground pepper

Almond Meatballs: Preheat oven to 350°F (175°C). Line a baking sheet with parchment paper. Heat olive oil in a small frying pan on medium. Add onion and garlic and cook for about 5 minutes until softened.

Add cumin, pepper and cinnamon, and cook for about 1 minute until fragrant. Scrape into a large bowl.

Add next 7 ingredients and mix well to combine. Roll tablespoons of mixture into balls and place on prepared baking sheet. Cook in preheated oven for about 20 minutes, turning once during cooking, until browned and cooked through.

Yogurt Dipping Sauce: Combine all 5 ingredients in a small bowl. Serve meatballs with yogurt dipping sauce.

1 meatball with 1 tsp (5 mL) dipping sauce:
45 Calories; 2.5 g Total Fat (1 g Mono, 0 g Poly, 0.5 g Sat); 10 mg Cholesterol; 3 g Carbohydrate; 0 g Fibre; 3 g Protein; 20 mg Sodium

Make-ahead Tip

The meatballs can be prepared 2 days ahead; store, covered, in the refrigerator. If you want to freeze them, place on a baking sheet, cover with plastic wrap and freeze until solid. Once frozen, transfer to sealable freezer bags. Thaw completely in a single layer on a baking sheet before cooking.

CHEESE QUESADILLAS WITH LIME PEACH SALSA

Makes 36 wedges and about 1 1/2 cups (375 mL) salsa; serves 8 to 10

Quesadilla wedges are best served hot while they are still crisp with the cheese melting. To keep them warm while you are cooking the remaining ones, put them on a wire rack on a baking sheet and place, uncovered, in a warm oven (200°F, 95°C).

CHEESE QUESADILLAS

2 cups (500 mL) grated jalapeño Monterey Jack cheese

1/2 cup (125 mL) sour cream

6 large flour tortillas

LIME PEACH SALSA

14 oz (398 mL) can peach halves in natural juice, drained, finely chopped

2 ripe medium tomatoes, quartered, seeded, finely chopped

1/3 cup (75 mL) finely chopped red onion

2 garlic cloves, minced

2 Tbsp (30 mL) finely chopped fresh cilantro

2 Tbsp (30 mL) lime juice

1 tsp (5 mL) hot pepper sauce

1/4 tsp (1 mL) salt

Cheese Quesadillas: Combine cheese and sour cream in a small bowl. Spread half of 1 side of each tortilla with cheese mixture. Fold other half over to cover filling. Press down lightly to seal. Heat a large frying pan on medium until hot. Cook quesadillas for 2 to 3 minutes on each side until golden brown and crisp. Cut each into 6 wedges.

Lime Peach Salsa: Combine all 8 ingredients in a medium bowl. Serve immediately or cover and chill for 1 to 3 hours before serving to allow flavour to develop. Serve quesadilla wedges with lime peach salsa.

1 wedge and 2 tsp (10 mL) salsa: 50 Calories; 2.5 g Total Fat (0 g Mono, 0 g Poly, 1.5 g Sat); 5 mg Cholesterol; 6 g Carbohydrate; 0 g Fibre; 2 g Protein; 125 mg Sodium

Make-ahead Tip

Quesadillas can be made a day ahead; store, wrapped in plastic wrap, in the refrigerator. They can be frozen for 1 month and thawed in refrigerator before cooking.

GRILLED BRIE AND FRUIT CROSTINI

Makes 24; serves 6 to 8

*What an impressive appetizer! And it's really simple to put together.
The salsa also works well as an accompaniment for chicken, fish or pork.*

1/2 cup (125 mL) canned white kidney beans, drained, rinsed and coarsely chopped

1/2 cup (125 mL) diced mango

1/2 cup (125 mL) diced red apple (with peel)

2 Tbsp (30 mL) finely chopped red onion

1 small hot pepper, seeded and finely diced (see p. 7), optional

2 Tbsp (30 mL) balsamic vinegar

1 Tbsp (15 mL) chopped fresh cilantro

1 Tbsp (15 mL) chopped fresh parsley

1 tsp (5 mL) granulated sugar

24 baguette bread slices, cut 1/2 inch (12 mm) thick

2 small brie cheese rounds (with rind), 4 oz. (113 g) each

1/4 cup (60 mL) olive (or canola) oil

Combine first 9 ingredients in a small bowl. Cover. Let stand at room temperature for 1 hour, stirring several times, to blend flavours.

Preheat lightly greased electric grill to medium. Lightly brush both sides of baguette slices and cheese rounds with olive oil. Place baguette slices on grill. Cook for about 1 minute, turning to toast both sides. Increase heat to medium-high. Place cheese rounds on grill. Cook for 4 to 5 minutes on each side, turning carefully, until soft to touch. Arrange on serving platter with fruity salsa and baguette slices.

Or, toast baguette slices on both sides under broiler. Heat cheese rounds in 325°F (160°C) oven for 5 to 10 minutes until softened.

1 crostini: 92 Calories; 5.6 g Total Fat (2.7 g Mono, 0.4 g Poly, 2.2 g Sat); 10 mg Cholesterol; 7 g Carbohydrate; 1 g Fibre; 3 g Protein; 133 mg Sodium

✳ *If you don't care for cilantro, omit the cilantro in this recipe and double the amount of chopped parsley.*

ARTICHOKE AND CHEESE DIP

Serves 4

Use an assortment of sliced vegetables, tortilla crisps or torn pieces of crusty bread for dipping.

14 oz (398 mL) can artichokes, drained and chopped

1 cup (250 mL) grated white Cheddar cheese

1/2 cup (125 mL) finely grated Parmesan cheese

1/4 cup (60 mL) mayonnaise

1/4 cup (60 mL) sour cream

1/4 cup (60 mL) thinly sliced green onion

1/4 tsp (1 mL) paprika

Preheat oven to 350°F (175°C). Grease a 2 to 3 cup (500 to 750 mL) ovenproof serving dish. Combine first 6 ingredients in a medium bowl. Spread into prepared dish.

Sprinkle with paprika. Bake in preheated oven for about 20 minutes until hot and bubbling around sides. Serve warm.

1 serving: 300 Calories; 26 g Total Fat (1.5 g Mono, 0 g Poly, 11 g Sat); 45 mg Cholesterol; 6 g Carbohydrate; 2 g Fibre; 12 g Protein; 640 mg Sodium

Make-ahead Tip
This dip can be prepared 1 or 2 days ahead; spread into an ovenproof serving dish, cover with plastic wrap and store in refrigerator. Remove from refrigerator 30 minutes before baking.

Roasted Pepper Tarts

Makes about 32; serves 8

This recipe uses mini muffin pans. You can use chopped fresh basil instead of parsley if you prefer. The tarts are best served warm.

2 medium red peppers, quartered, seeds and membranes removed

FILLING

3/4 cup (175 mL) sour cream

1/2 cup (125 mL) half-and-half cream

4 large eggs

1/3 cup (75 mL) finely grated Parmesan cheese

2 Tbsp (30 mL) chopped fresh parsley

1/4 tsp (1 mL) salt

1/4 tsp (1 mL) pepper

14 oz (397 g) package puff pastry, thawed according to package directions

Place peppers, skin-side up, on a baking sheet. Broil for about 5 minutes until skin is blistered and blackened. Place in a small bowl, cover with plastic wrap and let stand for 10 minutes. Peel peppers and finely chop.

Filling: Lightly grease mini muffin pans. Preheat oven to 350°F (175°C). Whisk next 7 ingredients in a medium bowl.

Roll half of pastry out on a lightly floured surface until about 13 inch (33 cm) square. Using 3 inch (7.5 cm) round cutter, cut 16 circles from 1 pastry half. Press rounds into prepared muffin pans. Repeat with remaining pastry half. Spoon about 1 tsp (5 mL) red pepper into each pastry case. Spoon about 2 tsp (10 mL) filling over pepper. Bake on bottom rack in preheated oven for 20 to 25 minutes until filling is set and pastry is golden. Serve warm.

1 tart: 100 Calories; 7 g Total Fat (3 g Mono, 0.5 g Poly, 2 g Sat); 20 mg Cholesterol; 7 g Carbohydrate; trace Fibre; 2 g Protein; 75 mg Sodium

Make-ahead Tip

The filling can be prepared a day ahead; store in a sealed container in the refrigerator. The tarts can be baked 1 to 3 hours ahead of time; reheat on baking sheets for about 10 to 12 minutes before serving.

GRILLED VEGETABLE PLATTER

Serves 6

This appetizer requires a little extra time for grilling the vegetables, but it is the perfect make-ahead appetizer—all you have to do when guests arrive is toast the bread. Vegetables can be cooked on a barbecue, electric grill or grill pan. You can add store-bought marinated artichokes and mushrooms to the platter along with a selection of deli meats. Remove grilled vegetables from the refrigerator 1 hour before serving.

SLOW-ROASTED TOMATOES

12 ripe medium Roma tomatoes, halved lengthwise

2 tsp (10 mL) granulated sugar

sprinkle of salt and pepper

GRILLED VEGETABLES

1 1/2 lbs (680 g) orange-fleshed sweet potatoes, peeled and cut lengthwise into 1/4 inch (6 mm) thick slices

1 medium eggplant, cut lengthwise into 1/4 inch (6 mm) thick slices

2 medium zucchini, cut lengthwise into 1/4 inch (6 mm) thick slices

1/4 cup (60 mL) olive oil

2 large red peppers, quartered, seeds and membranes removed

BALSAMIC MARINADE

3/4 cup (175 mL) olive oil

1/3 cup (75 mL) balsamic vinegar

1/4 cup (60 mL) finely grated Parmesan cheese

2 Tbsp (30 mL) chopped fresh oregano

2 Tbsp (30 mL) Thai sweet chili sauce

2 garlic cloves, minced

1 tsp (5 mL) brown sugar, packed

1/4 tsp (1 mL) salt

1/4 tsp (1 mL) pepper

TOASTS

1 to 2 loaves crusty bread, such as ciabatta

3 Tbsp (45 mL) olive oil

2 garlic cloves, halved

Slow-roasted Tomatoes: Preheat oven to 250°F (120°C). Grease a wire rack and place on a baking sheet. Place tomatoes, cut-side up, on wire rack. Sprinkle with sugar, salt and pepper. Roast in preheated oven for about 4 hours until semi-dried. Let cool, then transfer to a large sealable container.

Grilled Vegetables: Grease grill and preheat to medium. Brush both sides of sweet potato, eggplant and zucchini lightly with olive oil. Cook on preheated grill for 3 to 8 minutes on each side until softened and grill marks appear; place in container with tomatoes. Set aside.

Cook peppers on grill, skin-side down, until skin is blistered and blackened (or broil peppers in oven, skin-side up, for about 5 minutes). Place in a small bowl, cover with plastic wrap and let stand for 10 minutes. Peel and chop peppers into 1/2 inch (12 mm) thick strips; add to other vegetables.

Balsamic Marinade: Place all 9 ingredients in jar and shake well to combine. Drizzle vegetables with balsamic marinade and toss to coat. Seal and refrigerate for 8 hours or overnight.

Toasts: Preheat oven to 350°F (175°C). Cut bread into 1/2 inch (12 mm) thick slices, and brush both sides of each slice lightly with olive oil. Arrange in a single layer on a baking sheet. Toast in preheated oven for about 10 minutes, turning once, until lightly golden. Rub garlic clove over one side of each piece of bread. Serve bread with marinated vegetables.

1 serving: 660 Calories; 36 g Total Fat (25 g Mono, 4 g Poly, 6 g Sat); trace Cholesterol; 76 g Carbohydrate; 14 g Fibre; 11 g Protein; 420 mg Sodium

Make-ahead Tip

The vegetables can be made 3 days ahead and stored in a sealed container in the refrigerator. Turn container several times to allow all vegetables to be evenly coated in marinade.

Spicy Antipasto

Makes about 8 cups (2 L)

*Antipasto makes a great gift—arrange a jar of it in a basket, add some
delicious deli breads or crackers, some cheese and a bottle of wine and you
have a perfect Christmas gift for a host, friend or neighbour.*

2 cups (500 mL) chopped
cauliflower florets

2 cups (500 mL) chopped
red pepper

14 oz (398 mL) can artichoke
hearts, drained and
chopped

14 oz (398 mL) can tomato
sauce

10 oz (284 mL) jar pickled
mushrooms, drained and
chopped

1 cup (250 mL) chopped
pickled onions

1 cup (250 mL) red wine
vinegar

1/2 cup (125 mL) thinly
sliced stuffed green olives

1/2 cup (125 mL) brown
sugar, packed

1/3 cup (75 mL) thinly sliced
pitted kalamata olives

4 garlic cloves, minced

1 Tbsp (15 mL) hot pepper
sauce

2 tsp (10 mL) dried crushed
chilies

1/4 tsp (1 mL) salt

1/2 tsp (2 mL) pepper

2 x 6 oz (170 g) cans tuna
packed in spring water,
flaked

1/4 cup (60 mL) chopped
fresh basil

Combine first 15 ingredients in a large pot or Dutch oven.
Bring to a boil, then reduce heat to medium-low. Simmer,
uncovered, for about 20 minutes, stirring occasionally,
until thickened.

Stir in tuna and basil. Spoon mixture into hot, sterilized jars
and seal.

*1/4 cup (60 mL) antipasto: 50 Calories; 1.5 g Total Fat (0.5 g Mono,
0 g Poly, 0 g Sat); trace Cholesterol; 7 g Carbohydrate; 1 g Fibre;
3 g Protein; 310 mg Sodium*

Make-ahead Tip

The antipasto can be made 4 weeks ahead; store in sealed
containers in the refrigerator. Once open, use within 1 week.

ALMOND CRISPS WITH PORT AND CRANBERRY CHUTNEY

Serves 6

The sweetness of the chutney makes a perfect partner to a creamy cheese such as Cambozola or brie. The recipe is completely make-ahead, but remember to take the cheese and chutney out of the refrigerator 1 hour before serving to allow them to soften.

ALMOND CRISPS

2 egg whites (large)

1/3 cup (75 mL) granulated sugar

1 cup (250 mL) all-purpose flour

1/2 tsp (2 mL) pepper

1/4 tsp (1 mL) ground cinnamon

1/4 tsp (1 mL) ground nutmeg

1/4 tsp (1 mL) salt

1 cup (250 mL) whole almonds

PORT AND CRANBERRY CHUTNEY

3 cups (750 mL) port

1 1/2 cups (375 mL) dried cranberries, coarsely chopped

1/4 cup (60 mL) brown sugar, packed

2 tsp (10 mL) balsamic vinegar

1/4 tsp (1 mL) salt

Almond Crisps: Grease an 8 x 4 x 2 inch (20 x 10 x 5 cm) loaf pan. Preheat oven to 325°F (160°C). Using electric mixer, beat egg whites and sugar in a medium bowl for about 3 minutes until mixture is white and thick.

Stir in next 5 ingredients; mix well. Stir in almonds. Spoon into prepared pan and smooth top. Bake in preheated oven for about 35 minutes until lightly browned around edges; cool in pan for 1 hour. Turn out onto cutting board and cut into 1/8 inch (3 mm) thick slices. Place slices in single layer on ungreased baking sheets. Bake in preheated oven for about 15 minutes until crisp and lightly golden; cool completely before storing.

Port and Cranberry Chutney: Combine all 5 ingredients in a medium saucepan and stir on medium until sugar is dissolved. Boil gently for about 15 minutes, stirring occasionally, until thickened. Chutney will continue to thicken as it cools. Serve crisps with chutney.

1 serving: 590 Calories; 16 g Total Fat (0 g Mono, 0 g Poly, 1 g Sat); 0 mg Cholesterol; 75 g Carbohydrate; 5 g Fibre; 9 g Protein; 220 mg Sodium

Make-ahead Tip
The crisps can be made 4 days ahead; store in a sealed container in a cool place. The chutney can be made a week ahead; store in a sealed container in the refrigerator.

SPICED NUT NIBBLE MIX

Makes about 3 cups (750 mL)

Use your favourite nuts—or a variety!—for this recipe. This nut mix can easily be doubled or tripled if you want to give some away as gifts.

1 egg white (large)

1/3 cup (75 mL) granulated sugar

1 tsp (5 mL) cayenne pepper

1 tsp (5 mL) ground cumin

1/2 tsp (2 mL) salt

1/2 tsp (2 mL) pepper

1/4 tsp (1 mL) ground cinnamon

1 cup (250 mL) cashews

1 cup (250 mL) pecans

1 cup (250 mL) whole almonds

Preheat oven to 375°F (190°C). Line a baking sheet with parchment paper. Whisk first 7 ingredients in a large bowl.

Add all nuts and stir to coat. Spread mixture on prepared baking sheet. Cook in preheated oven, stirring occasionally, for about 30 minutes until nuts are golden. Mixture will become crisp as the nuts cool. Cool completely before storing.

1/3 cup (75 mL) nut mix: 320 Calories; 24 g Total Fat (8 g Mono, 4 g Poly, 2.5 g Sat); 0 mg Cholesterol; 18 g Carbohydrate; 4 g Fibre; 8 g Protein; 135 mg Sodium

Make-ahead Tip

Nut mix can be made 2 weeks ahead; store in a sealed container in cool, dry place.

SENSATIONAL SEAFOOD SOUP

Serves 6

You can remove the cooked mussel meat from the shells before serving if you like, but the shells make such a nice presentation that we prefer to serve the mussels still in their shells. This hearty stew-like soup is great as a starter, and would also make a delicious light main course served with crusty bread and a green salad.

1 Tbsp (15 mL) olive oil

1 cup (250 mL) chopped onion

1 cup (250 mL) finely chopped red pepper

4 garlic cloves, minced

28 oz (796 mL) can diced tomatoes (with juice)

2 cups (500 mL) chicken broth

1 cup (250 mL) white wine

1/4 cup (60 mL) tomato paste

1 tsp (5 mL) granulated sugar

(continued on next page)

Heat olive oil in a large pot or Dutch oven on medium. Add onion and red pepper and cook for about 10 minutes, stirring occasionally, until softened. Add garlic and cook for about 3 minutes until softened and fragrant.

Add tomatoes with their juice, chicken broth, wine, tomato paste, sugar, salt and pepper. Bring to a boil, then reduce heat to medium-low. Simmer, uncovered, for 10 minutes, stirring occasionally.

Put mussels into medium bowl. Lightly tap to close any that are opened 1/4 inch (6 mm) or more. Discard any that do not close (see Note). Add mussels and cod to tomato mixture. Cook, covered, for about 3 minutes until mussels are opened and cod flakes easily when tested with a fork. Discard any mussels that do not open. Add shrimp. Cook for about 2 minutes until shrimp just start to turn pink. Gently stir in scallops. Cook for 1 to 2 minutes until just opaque. Serve immodiatcly.

1 serving: 200 Calories; 4.5 g Total Fat (2 g Mono, 1 g Poly, 1 g Sat); 135 mg Cholesterol; 18 g Carbohydrate; 2 g Fibre; 34 g Protein; 1140 mg Sodium

Note: For safety reasons, it is important to discard any mussels that do not close when tapped before cooking, as well as any that have not opened during cooking.

1/2 tsp (2 mL) salt

1/2 tsp (2 mL) pepper

1/2 lb (225 g) mussels, scrubbed clean if necessary

3/4 lb (340 g) cod or halibut, cut into 1/2 inch (12 mm) pieces

11 oz (310 g) bay uncooked medium shrimp (peeled and deveined), halved crosswise

1/2 lb (225 g) scallops

FRENCH ONION SOUP

Serves 6

Cooking the onions for so long sweetens and mellows their flavour.

1 Tbsp (15 mL) olive oil

6 cups (1.5 L) thinly sliced onions

Heat olive oil in a large pot or Dutch oven on medium-low. Add onions and cook, covered, for about 45 minutes, stirring occasionally, until very soft and brown.

4 cups (1 L) beef broth

1 cup (250 mL) dry sherry

1 bay leaf

1 sprig fresh thyme

salt and pepper, to taste

Stir in next 4 ingredients. Cover and bring to a boil. Reduce heat to low. Simmer for 20 minutes, stirring occasionally, to allow flavours to develop. Remove bay leaf and thyme. Season with salt and pepper. Pour into 6 ovenproof dishes.

3 cups (750 mL) cubed (3/4 inch, 2 cm, pieces) baguette

2 cups (500 mL) grated Gruyère cheese

Top with bread, then sprinkle with cheese. Broil for 1 to 2 minutes until cheese is melted.

1 serving: 310 Calories; 14 g Total Fat (5 g Mono, 1 g Poly, 7 g Sat); 40 mg Cholesterol; 21 g Carbohydrate; 2 g Fibre; 15 g Protein; 660 mg Sodium

Make-ahead Tip

The soup can be made 1 to 2 days in advance; refrigerate in a sealed container. Reheat before spooning into serving dishes and topping with bread cubes and cheese.

ROASTED SWEET POTATO SOUP

Serves 6

Alongside thick, crusty bread, this soup makes a perfect starter for Christmas Day or a cold wintery night. Roasting the sweet potatoes helps to caramelize them, sweetening their flavour.

3 lbs (1.4 kg) orange-fleshed sweet potatoes, peeled and cut into 1 inch (2.5 cm) cubes

1 Tbsp (15 mL) olive oil

1/2 tsp (2 mL) ground cumin

1/4 tsp (1 mL) cayenne pepper

1/4 tsp (1 mL) salt

1/4 tsp (1 mL) pepper

1 Tbsp (15 mL) olive oil

1 cup (250 mL) chopped onion

2 garlic cloves, minced

6 cups (1.5 L) chicken broth

1 cup (250 mL) whipping cream

salt and pepper, to taste

Grease a baking sheet. Preheat oven to 375°F (190°C). Combine first 6 ingredients on prepared baking sheet. Roast in preheated oven for about 50 minutes, stirring occasionally, until softened and lightly browned.

Heat second amount of oil in a large pot or Dutch oven on medium-high. Add onion and cook for about 10 minutes, stirring occasionally, until onion is softened and browned (browning the onion helps to give the soup its flavour). Add garlic and cook for about 2 minutes until fragrant. Add sweet potato and chicken broth and stir. Carefully process in blender in 3 to 4 batches until smooth. Return mixture to same pot and bring to a boil, then reduce heat to medium-low.

Add whipping cream and stir until well combined and hot. Season to taste with salt and pepper.

1 serving: 380 Calories; 17 g Total Fat (7 g Mono, 1 g Poly, 9 g Sat); 45 mg Cholesterol; 53 g Carbohydrate; 7 g Fibre; 5 g Protein; 800 mg Sodium

Make-ahead Tip

Soup can be made 1 to 3 days ahead; store in a sealed container in the refrigerator. To reheat, place in a large pot or Dutch oven and stir on medium-low until hot.

CREAMY MUSHROOM SOUP

Serves 6

Dried mushrooms give the soup a deep, earthy flavour. They are available in most grocery stores or in specialty food stores.

3/4 oz (22 g) package dried porcini mushrooms

2 Tbsp (30 mL) butter

1 Tbsp (15 mL) olive oil

2 lbs (900 g) brown or white mushrooms, thinly sliced (about 10 cups, 2.5 L)

1 cup (250 mL) sliced green onion

4 garlic cloves, minced

1/3 cup (75 mL) dry sherry

1/4 cup (60 mL) all-purpose flour

1/4 tsp (1 mL) salt

1/4 tsp (1 mL) pepper

4 cups (1 L) chicken broth

3/4 cup (175 mL) whipping cream

Place porcini mushrooms in a small heatproof bowl and cover with warm water. Let stand for 20 minutes; drain. Coarsely chop, discarding any tough stems; set aside.

Heat butter and oil in a large pot or Dutch oven on medium. Add mushrooms, green onion and garlic and cook for about 10 minutes, stirring occasionally, until softened.

Stir in next 4 ingredients. Cook for 1 minute, stirring.

Gradually stir in broth and porcini mushrooms. Increase heat to high and bring to a boil, then reduce heat to low. Simmer, covered, for about 20 minutes until slightly thickened; cool slightly. Remove 2 cups (500 mL) of mixture and set aside. Carefully process remaining mixture in blender in 2 or 3 batches until smooth. Return mixture to same pot.

Add cream and reserved mushroom mixture and stir on medium until hot.

1 serving: 240 Calories; 16 g Total Fat (5 g Mono, 1 g Poly, 9 g Sat); 45 mg Cholesterol; 17 g Carbohydrate; 2 g Fibre; 6 g Protein; 520 mg Sodium

Silky Butternut Squash Soup

Makes about 16 cups (4 L); serves 12

'Tis in season, so there's no better time to serve butternut squash. It's perfectly partnered with leek and potatoes in this rich, velvety-textured soup. Garnish with fresh chopped chives.

1 Tbsp (15 mL) canola oil

1 1/2 cups (375 mL) thinly sliced leek (white part only)

1 Tbsp (15 mL) ground ginger

3 garlic cloves, minced (or 3/4 tsp, 4 mL, powder)

10 cups (2.5 L) chopped peeled butternut squash (see p. 7)

8 cups (2 L) chicken broth

4 1/2 cups (1.1 L) chopped peeled potato

1/2 tsp (2 mL) pepper

Heat canola oil in a large pot or Dutch oven on medium. Add leek, ginger and garlic. Stir. Cook for about 5 minutes, stirring often, until leek is softened.

Add remaining 4 ingredients. Stir. Bring to a boil. Reduce heat to medium-low. Simmer, covered, for about 20 minutes, stirring occasionally, until squash and potato are softened. Remove from heat. Let stand for about 10 minutes until slightly cooled. Process squash mixture with hand blender (or in blender or food processor in small batches) until smooth. Heat and stir on medium for about 5 minutes until heated through.

1 serving: 130 Calories; 1.5 g Total Fat (0.5 g Mono, 0 g Poly, 0 g Sat); 0 mg Cholesterol; 29 g Carbohydrate; 3 g Fibre; 3 g Protein; 380 mg Sodium

Make-ahead Tip
The soup may be stored in an airtight container in the freezer for up to 1 month. Thaw overnight in the refrigerator. To reheat slowly, cook in a 4 to 5 quart (4 to 5 L) slow cooker on Low for 4 hours or on High for 2 hours. To reheat the soup more quickly, heat in a large pot or Dutch oven on medium for about 30 minutes, stirring occasionally, until heated through.

Roast Beef with Horseradish and Bacon Stuffing

Serves 16

You can substitute broth or red wine for the port, although you won't achieve quite the same flavour. If a large roast is not available in the meat section, ask the butcher to cut one for you.

HORSERADISH AND BACON STUFFING

4 bacon slices, chopped

1 Tbsp (15 mL) canola oil

1 cup (250 mL) finely chopped onion

2 cups (500 mL) fine fresh bread crumbs (see p. 7)

3 Tbsp (45 mL) chopped fresh parsley

2 Tbsp (30 mL) creamed horseradish

1 large egg, fork-beaten

ROAST BEEF

6 lb (2.7 kg) beef sirloin roast

sprinkle of salt and pepper

GRAVY

1/4 cup (60 mL) all-purpose flour

4 cups (1 L) beef broth

1 cup (250 mL) port

1/4 cup (60 mL) creamed horseradish

2/3 cup (150 mL) whipping cream

1/4 tsp (1 mL) salt

Horseradish and Bacon Stuffing: Cook bacon in a medium frying pan on medium for about 5 minutes until golden brown. Drain on paper towel, chop finely and place in a large bowl. Discard bacon fat from pan. Heat canola oil in same pan on medium. Add onion and cook for about 5 minutes until softened. Add to bacon. Add remaining 4 ingredients and stir until well combined.

Roast Beef: Preheat oven to 350°F (175°C). Grease a wire rack and place in a roasting pan. Cut roast in half horizontally almost but not quite through to the other side. Open flat. Spread 1 side of roast with horseradish and bacon stuffing. Fold other side over to enclose stuffing. Using butcher's twine, tie roast at 1 inch (2.5 cm) intervals. Sprinkle with salt and pepper. Place in prepared pan. Pour 1 cup (250 mL) water into pan. Roast, uncovered, in preheated oven for 1 hour, then turn over. Roast, uncovered, for 1 1/2 hours until a meat thermometer inserted into thickest part of roast (not stuffing) reads 155°F (68°C) for medium or until desired doneness. Let stand, covered, for 20 minutes before cutting into 1/2 inch (12 mm) thick slices. Reserve 1/2 cup (125 mL) pan drippings.

Gravy: Heat reserved pan drippings in the same roasting pan on medium. Add flour and cook for about 1 minute until thickened. Slowly stir in broth, whisking to remove any lumps. Stir in port and horseradish. Boil gently for about 10 minutes, stirring occasionally, until thickened. Add whipping cream and salt and stir until hot. Strain to remove any lumps. Serve roast beef with stuffing and gravy.

1 serving: 500 Calories; 21 g Total Fat (8 g Mono, 1 g Poly, 9 g Sat); 105 mg Cholesterol; 17 g Carbohydrate; trace Fibre; 37 g Protein; 510 mg Sodium

Make-ahead Tip

Stuffing can be prepared a day ahead; store in a sealed container in the refrigerator. Stuffing can also be frozen up to 1 month ahead; freeze in sealable bag. Note that the stuffing compacts when frozen and thawed. Let stuffing thaw completely before stuffing beef.

Glazed Ham

Serves 18

You might have to order a ham this large from a butcher or specialty food store. If you are cooking a smaller ham without the rind, halve the glaze recipe, brush it over the ham and proceed with cooking and basting as instructed. Choose from one of our two glazes.

20 lb (9 kg) leg of cooked ham with rind

whole cloves (optional)

APRICOT GLAZE

1 cup (250 mL) pineapple juice

1/2 cup (125 mL) apricot jam

2 Tbsp (30 mL) grainy mustard

MAPLE ORANGE GLAZE

3/4 cup (175 mL) maple syrup

1/3 cup (75 mL) marmalade

1/3 cup (75 mL) orange juice

1 Tbsp (15 mL) Worcestershire sauce

Preheat oven to 350°F (175°C). Grease a wire rack and place in a roasting pan. Cut through rind at shank end of leg. Run your fingers under rind to loosen. Carefully pull away rind, using fingers. Discard rind. Make shallow cuts, about 1 inch (2.5 cm) apart, in 1 direction diagonally across fat. Make sure cuts aren't too deep or you will lose the decorative pattern. Then make shallow cuts in the opposite direction to form a diamond pattern.

Place 1 clove where each cut meets at the tip of each diamond shape. Place ham in prepared pan. Wrap a piece of greased foil around bone-end. Brush ham with your choice of glaze. Bake, uncovered, in preheated oven for about 1 hour, brushing frequently with glaze, until browned and glazed. Carve into thin slices. Serve hot or cold.

Apricot Glaze: Stir all 3 ingredients in a small saucepan on medium until jam is melted.

Maple Orange Glaze: Stir all 4 ingredients in a small saucepan on medium until marmalade is melted.

1 serving with apricot glaze: 900 Calories; 42 g Total Fat (20 g Mono, 5 g Poly, 14 g Sat); 290 mg Cholesterol; 9 g Carbohydrate; 0 g Fibre; 112 g Protein; 4910 mg Sodium

Make-ahead Tip

The ham can be cooked a day or two ahead; serve cold. Or, prepare the ham a day or two ahead by scoring it and inserting cloves. Place in baking dish, cover and refrigerate. Remove from the refrigerator 1 hour before cooking. Remove the cover before cooking. The glazes can be made a day ahead; store at room temperature in a sealed container.

BACON AND ROSEMARY ROASTED PORK

Serves 16

*Make sure you have some butcher's twine
on hand to tie around the pork.*

6 lb (2.7 kg) pork loin roast

4 garlic cloves, peeled and quartered

3 Tbsp (45 mL) Dijon mustard

1/4 tsp (1 mL) salt

1/4 tsp (1 mL) pepper

8 large sprigs fresh rosemary

8 to 10 bacon slices

APPLE MUSTARD GRAVY

1/3 cup (75 mL) all-purpose flour

3 cups (750 mL) chicken broth

1 1/2 cups (375 mL) apple juice

1 Tbsp (15 mL) Dijon mustard

salt and pepper, to taste

Preheat oven to 350°F (175°C). Lightly grease a wire rack and place in a roasting pan. Make 16 slits evenly all over pork and insert a piece of garlic into each slit.

Spread mustard evenly over pork. Sprinkle with salt and pepper. Lay rosemary sprigs lengthwise on top of pork. Wrap bacon around pork. Secure pork with butcher's twine tied at 1 inch (2.5 cm) intervals. Place in prepared pan. Roast, uncovered, in preheated oven for 2 1/2 to 3 hours until meat thermometer inserted into thickest part of roast reads 150°F (65°C). Do not overcook. Cover with foil. Reserve pan drippings. Let pork stand for 20 minutes before carving into 1/2 inch (12 mm) thick slices.

Apple Mustard Gravy: Heat reserved drippings in same roasting pan on medium. Add flour and cook for about 1 minute until thickened. Gradually stir in chicken broth and apple juice, whisking to remove any lumps. Stir in mustard. Boil gently for about 5 to 10 minutes, stirring occasionally, until thickened. Strain and season to taste with salt and pepper. Serve pork with apple mustard gravy.

1 serving: 310 Calories; 15 g Total Fat (4 g Mono, 1 g Poly, 6 g Sat); 105 mg Cholesterol; 6 g Carbohydrate; 0 g Fibre; 36 g Protein; 850 mg Sodium

Make-ahead Tip
Pork can be prepared a day ahead; wrap well and store in the refrigerator. Let stand at room temperature for 1 hour before roasting.

LAMB AND RED WINE BRAISE

Serves 8

Whether you're entertaining over the festive season or feeding a hungry family, this recipe is certain to chase away those winter chills. You can use stewing beef in place of lamb if you prefer.

1/4 cup (60 mL) all-purpose flour

4 lbs (1.8 kg) lamb stewing meat, such as leg or shoulder, cut into 3/4 inch (2 cm) pieces

2 Tbsp (30 mL) olive oil

1 Tbsp (15 mL) olive oil

1 1/2 cups (375 mL) coarsely chopped carrot

1 1/2 cups (375 mL) coarsely chopped onion

2 cups (500 mL) sliced mushrooms

4 garlic cloves, minced

1 1/2 cups (375 mL) red wine

1 cup (250 mL) chicken broth

1/4 cup (60 mL) tomato paste

4 small sprigs fresh rosemary

1/2 tsp (2 mL) salt

1/2 tsp (2 mL) pepper

Toss flour and lamb in batches in a large plastic bag until lamb is coated. Heat first amount of olive oil in a large pot or Dutch oven on medium-high. Add lamb in 3 to 4 batches and sear until browned all over; remove from pan. Add a little more oil if necessary for browning.

Heat second amount of olive oil in same pot on medium. Add carrot and onion and cook for about 5 minutes until onion is softened. Add mushrooms and garlic and cook for about 5 minutes until mushrooms are softened.

Stir in lamb and remaining 6 ingredients. Bring to a boil, then reduce heat to low. Cook, covered, for 1 hour, stirring occasionally. Remove cover and cook for 30 to 45 minutes, stirring occasionally, until lamb is tender and sauce is thickened.

1 serving: 440 Calories; 17 g Total Fat (9 g Mono, 1.5 g Poly, 5 g Sat); 145 mg Cholesterol; 12 g Carbohydrate; 2 g Fibre; 48 g Protein; 410 mg Sodium

Make-ahead Tip
This recipe can be made a day ahead; store in a sealed
container in the refrigerator. Reheat slowly in a large pot on
low until hot. It can also be frozen in a sealed container for
up to 1 month. Thaw in refrigerator before reheating.

TOURTIÈRES

Makes 12

These tasty miniature pies are delicious served with spicy ketchup.

1 Tbsp (15 mL) canola oil
1 cup (250 mL) finely chopped onion
4 garlic cloves, minced
1 tsp (5 mL) ground allspice

3/4 lb (340 g) ground beef
3/4 lb (340 g) ground pork
1/2 tsp (2 mL) salt
1 tsp (5 mL) pepper

1/2 cup (125 mL) beef (or chicken) broth
2/3 cup (150 mL) fine dry bread crumbs, toasted

17 oz (540 g) package flaky pie crust mix
2/3 cup (150 mL) water

1 large egg, fork-beaten
1 Tbsp (15 mL) milk

Grease a 12-cup muffin pan. Heat canola oil in a large frying pan on medium. Add onion and cook for about 5 minutes until softened. Add garlic and allspice and cook for about 1 minute until fragrant.

Stir in beef, pork, salt and pepper. Cook, breaking up pieces of ground meat, until browned.

Add broth and stir. Cook, uncovered, for 5 to 10 minutes until almost all broth is evaporated. Remove from heat and stir in bread crumbs; cool.

Preheat oven to 400°F (200°C). Combine both envelopes of pastry mix and water in a large bowl and stir until soft dough forms. Press dough together. Roll out two-thirds of dough on lightly floured surface to 1/8 inch (3 mm) thickness. Cut twelve 4 1/2 inch (11 cm) circles from pastry. Press into prepared muffin pan, leaving a slight overhang of pastry at top. Press 1/3 cup (75 mL) ground meat mixture into each pastry case. Roll remaining pastry onto lightly floured surface until pastry is 1/8 inch (3 mm) thick. Cut twelve 3 1/2 inch (9 cm) circles from pastry. Place over ground meat mixture. Press edges of pastry together to seal and tuck edges under. Lightly press around edges using a lightly floured fork to seal.

Whisk egg and milk together in small bowl. Brush over pastry tops. Cut 3 slits into each pastry top. Bake on bottom shelf in preheated oven for about 35 minutes until pastry is golden and crisp. Let stand in pan for 5 minutes before serving.

1 tourtière: 400 Calories; 24 g Total Fat (12 g Mono, 2.5 g Poly, 7 g Sat); 50 mg Cholesterol; 27 g Carbohydrate; trace Fibre; 15 g Protein; 510 mg Sodium

Make-ahead Tip
The tourtières can be prepared 1 month ahead; freeze in a sealed container. Thaw in refrigerator before baking.

Herb Butter Turkey

Serves 6

Your Christmas feast will be a sure hit with this succulent turkey stuffed with pine nuts and dried apricots and served with cranberry gravy.

PINE NUT AND APRICOT STUFFING

6 bacon slices, chopped

1 cup (250 mL) chopped onion

1/2 cup (125 mL) chopped celery

1/2 cup (125 mL) finely chopped dried apricots

1 loaf day-old bread, crusts removed and diced (about 6 cups, 1.5 L)

1/2 cup (125 mL) pine nuts, toasted (see p. 8)

1/4 cup (60 mL) chopped fresh parsley

1/4 cup (60 mL) cranberry jelly

2 tsp (10 mL) finely grated orange zest

salt and pepper, to taste

TURKEY

10 lb (4.5 kg) turkey

1/2 cup (125 mL) butter, softened

2 tsp (10 mL) chopped fresh thyme

1 tsp (5 mL) celery salt

1/4 tsp (1 mL) pepper

2 garlic cloves, minced

(continued on next page)

Pine Nut and Apricot Stuffing: Cook bacon in a small frying pan on medium until golden; drain on paper towel. Drain and discard all but 2 tsp (10 mL) drippings. Cook onion and celery in reserved fat in same pan on medium for about 5 minutes until softened; scrape into a large bowl. Add bacon and remaining 8 ingredients. Mix well.

Turkey: Preheat oven to 350°F (175°C). Lightly grease a wire rack and place in a roasting pan. Remove and discard neck, giblets and any fat from turkey cavities. Rinse inside and out with cold water; pat dry with paper towels.

Combine next 5 ingredients in a small bowl. Using your fingers, carefully loosen turkey skin across breast and legs to separate skin from meat, trying not to pierce skin. Evenly spread butter mixture between skin and meat; smooth skin. Tuck wings under body. Fill body and neck cavity with stuffing. Secure openings with toothpicks or skewers. Tie legs together. Place in prepared pan.

Pour 1/2 cup (125 mL) water into pan. Cover turkey loosely with greased foil. Roast in preheated oven for 2 1/2 to 3 hours until a meat thermometer inserted into thickest part of thigh reaches 180°F (82°C). Temperature of stuffing should reach at least 165°F (74°C). Cover with foil; let stand for 20 minutes before carving and removing stuffing. Reserve 1/2 cup (125 mL) pan drippings for gravy.

Cranberry Gravy: Heat reserved pan drippings in same roasting pan on medium until bubbling. Add flour and cook for about 1 minute until thickened. Stir in brandy. Slowly stir in chicken broth and cranberry jelly, whisking to remove any lumps. Boil gently for about 10 minutes, stirring occasionally, until thickened. Add salt and pepper. Strain to remove any lumps. Serve turkey with cranberry gravy.

1 serving: 1210 Calories; 59 g Total Fat (18 g Mono, 13 g Poly, 21 g Sat); 300 mg Cholesterol; 65 g Carbohydrate; 5 g Fibre; 96 g Protein; 3920 mg Sodium

CRANBERRY GRAVY

1/4 cup (60 mL) all-purpose flour

1/4 cup (60 mL) brandy or chicken broth

3 cups (750 mL) chicken (or turkey) broth

1/2 cup (125 mL) cranberry jelly

salt and pepper, to taste

Make-ahead Tip

The stuffing can be made 1 month ahead; freeze in a sealed plastic bag or airtight container. Thaw stuffing before placing it into turkey. Stuff turkey just before cooking. Note that the stuffing compacts when frozen and thawed.

CORNISH HENS WITH PEAR STUFFING

Serves 6

These roasted hens would be delicious served with the cranberry gravy on page 65. If you make that gravy, reserve the same amount of pan juices from the hens as you would with the turkey.

PEAR STUFFING

1 Tbsp (15 mL) canola oil

1 cup (250 mL) finely chopped onion

1 1/2 cups (375 mL) finely chopped peeled pear

2 cups (500 mL) fresh fine bread crumbs (see p. 7)

1 cup (250 mL) walnuts, toasted (see p. 8), chopped

2 Tbsp (30 mL) chopped fresh sage

2 tsp (10 mL) balsamic vinegar

2 tsp (10 mL) brown sugar, packed

1/4 tsp (1 mL) salt

1/2 tsp (2 mL) pepper

CORNISH HENS

6 Cornish hens

salt and pepper, to taste

12 bacon slices

Pear Stuffing: Heat canola oil in a large frying pan on medium. Add onion and pear and cook for about 5 minutes until softened. Remove from heat. Add remaining 7 ingredients and mix until well combined.

Cornish Hens: Preheat oven to 350°F (175°C). Grease a wire rack and place in a roasting pan. Rinse hens inside and out under cold water and pat dry inside and out with paper towel. Fill each hen with about 1/2 cup (125 mL) pear stuffing. Secure opening with skewers and tie legs together with butcher's twine.

Sprinkle hens with salt and pepper. Wrap 2 slices of bacon around each hen. Place in prepared pan. Roast, uncovered, in preheated oven for 1 to 1 1/4 hours until a meat thermometer inserted in thickest part of each hen (not stuffing) reads 185°F (85°C). (Stuffing should reach 165°F, 74°C.) Cover with foil and let stand for 10 minutes.

1 serving: 700 Calories; 32 g Total Fat (9 g Mono, 13 g Poly, 6 g Sat); 235 mg Cholesterol; 40 g Carbohydrate; 5 g Fibre; 62 g Protein; 690 mg Sodium

Make-ahead Tip

The stuffing can be made 1 month ahead; store in a sealed
bag or container in the freezer. Thaw stuffing thoroughly
before placing it into hens. Stuff the hens just before cooking.
Note that the stuffing compacts when frozen and thawed.

ROAST GOOSE WITH BLACKBERRY PORT SAUCE

Serves 6

You can buy geese at grocery stores or specialty food stores. They are most commonly sold frozen. The stuffing for the Cornish Hens on page 66 would make a delicious stuffing for the goose.

ROAST GOOSE

8 lb (3.6 kg) goose

salt and pepper, to taste

BLACKBERRY PORT SAUCE

3 Tbsp (45 mL) all-purpose flour

1 cup (250 mL) port

2 cups (500 mL) chicken broth

1/3 cup (75 mL) blackberry jam

1/4 tsp (1 mL) salt

1/4 to 1/2 tsp (1 to 2 mL) pepper

Roast Goose: Preheat oven to 325°F (160°C). Grease a wire rack and place in a roasting pan. Remove and discard neck, giblets and any fat from goose cavities. Rinse goose inside and out with cold water. Pat dry with paper towels. Half fill a large pot, Dutch oven or steamer with water and bring to a boil. Wearing clean, heavy rubber gloves to protect your hands, place goose, neck cavity–side down, into boiling water and hold it there for 1 minute. Carefully turn goose and place other end into boiling water and hold for 1 minute. Remove from water. Place breast-side down in prepared pan; pat dry with paper towel. Let stand, uncovered, for 15 minutes until completely dry. Sprinkle with salt and pepper. Bake in preheated oven for 1 1/4 hours. Turn goose and cook for about 1 1/4 hours until skin is browned and a meat thermometer inserted in thigh reads 170°F (77°C). Cover with foil. Let stand for 20 minutes before carving. Pour pan drippings into a 2 cup (500 mL) measure. Let stand for 15 minutes. Pour off or spoon off fat and reserve 3 Tbsp (45 mL) drippings.

(continued on next page)

Blackberry Port Sauce: Heat reserved pan drippings in same roasting pan on medium-high. Add flour and cook for 1 minute. Slowly stir in port, whisking to remove any lumps. Add remaining 4 ingredients and stir until well combined. Boil gently, stirring occasionally, for about 10 minutes until thickened. Strain to remove any lumps.

1 serving: 610 Calories; 22 g Total Fat (6 g Mono, 2.5 g Poly, 8 g Sat); 255 mg Cholesterol; 20 g Carbohydrate; 0 g Fibre; 69 g Protein; 550 mg Sodium

Make-ahead Tip

The goose can be prepared a day ahead; store uncovered in the refrigerator. Leaving the goose uncovered helps to dry it, providing a crisper skin when roasted. Let stand at room temperature for 1 hour before roasting.

EASY CHICKEN CASSOULET

Serves 8

*Traditionally a cassoulet
(a dish of beans, poultry and/or meat)
takes almost 3 days to make and
contains duck or goose that has been
cooked in fat. This version takes a
fraction of the time, uses chicken
and canned beans and is
considerably lower in fat.*

1 Tbsp (15 mL) olive oil

12 skinless bone-in chicken thighs

4 Italian sausages

6 bacon slices

1 Tbsp (15 mL) olive oil

2 cups (500 mL) chopped onion

4 garlic cloves, minced

2 x 19 oz (540 mL) cans white kidney beans, rinsed and drained

2 cups (500 mL) chicken broth

1 cup (250 mL) white wine

1/4 cup (60 mL) tomato paste

1 Tbsp (15 mL) chopped fresh thyme

salt and pepper, to taste

1 1/2 cups (375 mL) fine fresh bread crumbs (see p. 7)

Preheat oven to 350°F (175°C). Grease a large casserole dish. Heat first amount of olive oil in a large pot or Dutch oven on medium-high. Add chicken in 2 batches and sear for about 10 minutes until browned all over; remove from pot. Cook sausages in same pot for about 10 minutes until browned all over. Remove from pot and cut into 1 inch (2.5 cm) pieces. Reduce heat to medium. Cook bacon in same pot until golden. Remove from pan and chop. Drain fat from pan.

Heat second amount of olive oil in same pot on medium. Add onion and cook for about 10 minutes until onion is softened. Add garlic and cook for about 2 minutes until fragrant.

Add next 5 ingredients and stir until well combined. Add chicken, sausage and bacon. Sprinkle with salt and pepper. Cover and bring to a boil. Spoon mixture into prepared dish. Cook, covered, in preheated oven for about 1 1/2 hours until sauce is thickened and chicken is very tender.

Sprinkle with bread crumbs and cook, uncovered, for 20 to 30 minutes until crumbs are golden and crisp.

1 serving: 630 Calories; 29 g Total Fat (13 g Mono, 4.5 g Poly, 9 g Sat); 115 mg Cholesterol; 45 g Carbohydrate; 13 g Fibre; 40 g Protein; 1060 mg Sodium

SEAFOOD POT PIES

Serves 4

These delicious pies are elegant as well as warming and homey. We used cod in this recipe, but you can use another type of fish such as halibut, monk fish or snapper, if you prefer.

1/2 x 17 oz (540 g) package flaky pie crust mix

1/3 cup (75 mL) water

2 Tbsp (30 mL) butter

1 leek (white part only), thinly sliced

3/4 cup (175 mL) finely chopped carrot

1/4 cup (60 mL) all-purpose flour

1/3 cup (75 mL) white wine (or milk)

1 2/3 cups (400 mL) milk

3/4 lb (340 g) cod, cut into 3/4 inch (2 cm) pieces

11 oz (310 g) medium uncooked shrimp (peeled and deveined), halved

8 oz (225 g) small scallops (or quartered large scallops), patted dry

1/2 cup (125 mL) frozen peas

1 egg yolk (large)

Combine pastry mix and water in a medium bowl and mix until a soft dough forms. Place on a lightly floured surface. Roll out to 1/4 inch (6 mm) thickness. Cut four 4 1/2 inch (11 cm) rounds from pastry. Cover and set aside.

Melt butter in a large saucepan on medium. Add leek and carrot and cook for about 5 minutes until leek is softened. Stir in flour and cook for 1 minute until grainy.

Stir in wine, then slowly add milk. Stir for about 10 minutes until mixture boils and thickens.

Add cod and shrimp and stir. Cook, covered, for about 5 minutes until seafood is almost cooked. Add scallops and peas and stir. Cook, covered, for about 3 minutes until scallops are just opaque; do not overcook. Remove from heat.

(continued on next page)

Preheat oven to 375°F (190°C). Spoon about 1 1/2 cups (375 mL) seafood mixture into 4 ramekins. Place a round of pastry over each ramekin and press around edge to seal. Brush pastry with egg yolk. Place ramekins on baking sheet to catch any filling that could spill out during baking. Bake in preheated oven for about 35 minutes until pastry is golden brown and crisp.

1 serving: 710 Calories; 29 g Total Fat (13 g Mono, 3.5 g Poly, 10 g Sat); 260 mg Cholesterol; 54 g Carbohydrate; 2 g Fibre; 53 g Protein; 910 mg Sodium

Make-ahead Tip

Pastry can be made, rolled out and cut a day ahead; store, covered, in refrigerator.

MAPLE-GLAZED SALMON

Serves 8

When you purchase the salmon, ask the store to remove the skin if you'd rather not do it yourself at home. This recipe was tested on a long cast-iron grill pan. If you don't have such a pan, either pan-fry the salmon in batches or broil it for 5 to 8 minutes per side.

1 cup (250 mL) maple syrup
1 cup (250 mL) olive oil
1/2 cup (125 mL) soy sauce
1 cup (250 mL) chopped fresh parsley
1/2 cup (125 mL) rye

3 lbs (1.4 kg) side of salmon, skin removed

Combine maple syrup, olive oil and soy sauce in a medium saucepan on medium-high. Bring to a boil and let boil for 3 minutes. Remove from heat and stir in parsley and rye. Let stand until cool.

Cut salmon into 6 to 8 pieces. Place in a large shallow baking dish. Pour marinade over and cover. Refrigerate for 12 to 24 hours, stirring occasionally.

Heat a long greased grill pan on medium using 2 burners or elements. Remove salmon from marinade; discard marinade. Pat salmon dry and place on grill pan. Cook for 5 to 8 minutes per side depending on thickness of salmon until salmon flakes easily when tested with a fork; do not overcook.

1 serving: 600 Calories; 38 g Total Fat (23 g Mono, 7 g Poly, 5 g Sat); 95 mg Cholesterol; 19 g Carbohydrate; 0 g Fibre; 36 g Protein; 1000 mg Sodium

Make-ahead Tip
Salmon can be marinated 2 days ahead; cover and store in the refrigerator.

VEGETARIAN LASAGNA

Serves 6

You can use 1 cup (250 mL) bottled pesto (such as sun-dried tomato or basil) in place of the parsley pesto if you prefer.

PARSLEY PESTO

1 cup (250 mL) fresh parsley sprigs

1/3 cup (75 mL) pine nuts, toasted (see p. 8)

1/4 cup (60 mL) grated Parmesan cheese

3 Tbsp (45 mL) olive oil

2 Tbsp (30 mL) water

1/4 tsp (1 mL) salt

WHITE SAUCE

3 Tbsp (45 mL) butter

1/4 cup (60 mL) all-purpose flour

2 cups (500 mL) milk

1/3 cup (75 mL) grated Parmesan cheese

1/4 tsp (1 mL) ground nutmeg

salt and pepper, to taste

LASAGNA

3 medium eggplants, cut lengthwise into 1/4 inch (6 mm) thick slices

1/4 cup (60 mL) olive oil

3 large red peppers, quartered, seeds and membranes removed

(continued on next page)

Parsley Pesto: Process all 6 ingredients in a food processor until smooth.

White Sauce: Melt butter in a medium saucepan on medium. Add flour and cook for 1 minute until grainy. Slowly stir in milk. Stir for about 5 minutes until mixture boils and thickens. Add next 4 ingredients and stir until well combined.

Lasagna: Lightly brush both sides of eggplant slices with first amount of olive oil. Grease and preheat barbecue or grill pan to medium-high. Cook eggplant on preheated grill for about 3 minutes per side until tender and grill marks appear. Set aside. Cook red peppers, skin-side down, on same grill until skin is blackened and blistered. Place in medium bowl and cover. Let stand for 10 minutes. Peel and cut into thin strips.

Heat second amount of olive oil in a large frying pan on medium-high. Add mushrooms and cook for about 5 minutes until lightly browned and softened.

Combine both cheeses in a small bowl.

Preheat oven to 350°F (175°C). To assemble, layer ingredients in greased 9 x 13 inch (23 x 33 cm) baking dish as follows:

1. 1 cup (250 mL) pasta sauce
2. 1/3 of lasagna sheets, breaking sheets where necessary to fit in dish
3. Mushrooms
4. 1 cup (250 mL) pasta sauce
5. Half of eggplant
6. Half of parsley pesto
7. Half of cheese mixture
8. 1/3 of lasagna sheets
9. Remaining pasta sauce
10. Red peppers

11. Remaining cheese mixture
12. Remaining eggplant
13. Remaining pesto
14. Remaining lasagna sheets

1 Tbsp (15 mL) olive oil

2 cups (500 mL) sliced mushrooms

1 cup (250 mL) grated mozzarella cheese

1/2 cup (125 mL) grated Parmesan cheese

22 oz (700 g) jar pasta sauce

20 instant lasagna sheets

Spread with white sauce; cover with foil. Bake in preheated oven for 30 minutes. Remove cover and bake for 45 to 55 minutes until browned around edges and lasagna sheets are tender when tested with skewer. Place under hot broiler for 3 to 5 minutes until golden brown. Cover and let stand for 15 minutes before cutting.

1 serving: 800 Calories; 42 g Total Fat (19 g Mono, 5 g Poly, 13 g Sat); 50 mg Cholesterol; 85 g Carbohydrate; 16 g Fibre; 29 g Protein; 1060 mg Sodium

Make-ahead Tip
Lasagna can be made 1 month ahead; cover and freeze. Let thaw before reheating, covered, in 350°F (175°C) oven for 30 to 40 minutes until hot.

VEGETABLE QUINOA CASSEROLE

Serves 6

A nutty oat crust holds delicious quinoa and vegetables in a curry-flavoured custard.

NUT CRUST

1 1/2 cups (375 mL)
quick-cooking rolled oats

1 cups (250 mL) all-purpose
flour

1/2 cup (125 mL) butter (or
hard margarine), softened

1/2 cup (125 mL) finely
chopped unsalted mixed
nuts, toasted (see p. 8)

2 Tbsp (30 mL) brown
sugar, packed

FILLING

1 cup (250 mL) vegetable
broth

1/8 tsp (0.5 mL) salt

2/3 cup (150 mL) quinoa,
rinsed and drained

2 tsp (10 mL) cooking oil

3 cups (750 mL) chopped
fresh white mushrooms

2 cups (500 mL) chopped
onion

2 garlic cloves, minced
(or 1/2 tsp, 2 mL, powder)

3 cups (750 mL) chopped
cauliflower

1 cup (250 mL) chopped red
pepper

(continued on next page)

Nut Crust: Preheat oven to 350°F (175°C). Mix first 5 ingredients in a medium bowl until mixture resembles coarse crumbs. Press firmly into bottom and halfway up sides of greased 3 quart (3 L) shallow baking dish. Bake in preheated oven for about 15 minutes until just golden. Let stand on wire rack to cool.

Filling: Combine vegetable broth and salt in a small saucepan. Bring to a boil. Add quinoa. Stir. Reduce heat to medium-low. Simmer, covered, for about 20 minutes, without stirring, until quinoa is tender and liquid is absorbed. Fluff with fork. Transfer to large bowl.

Heat cooking oil in a large frying pan on medium. Add mushrooms, onion and garlic. Cook for about 10 minutes, stirring often, until onion is softened. Add cauliflower, red pepper and carrot. Stir. Sprinkle with flour, curry powder, salt and pepper. Heat and stir for 1 minute. Add to quinoa. Stir. Let stand for 10 minutes.

Add cheeses. Stir.

Whisk eggs and milk in medium bowl until combined. Add to quinoa mixture. Stir. Pour into nut crust. Spread evenly. Bake in preheated oven for about 1 hour until knife inserted in centre comes out clean and top is golden. Let stand for 10 minutes before serving.

1 serving: 787 Calories; 43.4 g Total Fat (14.8 g Mono, 4.1 g Poly, 20.1 g Sat); 271 mg Cholesterol; 71 g Carbohydrate; 8 g Fibre; 32 g Protein; 751 mg Sodium

1 cup (250 mL) grated carrot

2 Tbsp (30 mL) all-purpose flour

2 tsp (10 mL) curry powder

1/2 tsp (2 mL) salt

1/4 tsp (1 mL) pepper

1 cup (250 mL) grated Gruyère cheese

1 cup (250 mL) grated sharp Cheddar cheese

6 large eggs

2 cups (500 mL) milk

GREEN BEANS WITH SAGE WALNUT BUTTER

Serves 6

If fresh beans are unavailable, use frozen whole beans.

3 Tbsp (45 mL) butter

1/3 cup (75 mL) walnuts, chopped

1 tsp (5 mL) chopped fresh sage

1 lb (454 g) green beans, stalk ends removed

Melt butter in a small saucepan on medium-low. Add walnuts and sage, and cook for about 5 minutes until butter is starting to turn golden brown.

Meanwhile, cook beans in a steamer in a large saucepan over simmering water for 5 to 8 minutes until bright green and tender. Drain water from pan and remove steamer. Add beans to same pan. Add butter mixture and toss to coat.

1 serving: 120 Calories; 10 g Total Fat (2 g Mono, 3.5 g Poly, 4 g Sat); 15 mg Cholesterol; 6 g Carbohydrate; 3 g Fibre; 2 g Protein; 45 mg Sodium

Make-ahead Tip

Remove stalk ends from beans a day ahead; store beans in a sealed bag in the refrigerator.

ROASTED BEET SALAD WITH MAPLE VINAIGRETTE

Serves 12

The earthy flavour of the beets and the sweetness of the pears make a delicious combination. This salad would also be really good sprinkled with some chopped toasted walnuts.

ROASTED BEET SALAD

8 medium beets, trimmed of stalks but unpeeled

2 ripe medium pears, peeled and thinly sliced

3 oz (85 g) goat (chèvre) cheese, coarsely crumbled

MAPLE VINAIGRETTE

1/4 cup (60 mL) maple syrup

3 Tbsp (45 mL) white vinegar

2 Tbsp (30 mL) olive oil

1/2 tsp (2 mL) salt

1/4 tsp (1 mL) pepper

Roasted Beet Salad: Preheat oven to 350°F (175°F). Wrap beets individually in foil (see p. 7). Place beets on a baking sheet. Roast in preheated oven for about 1 hour until beets are tender when pierced with skewer. Let stand for 10 to 15 minutes until cool enough to handle. Peel beets. Cut beets into wedges.

Arrange beets, pears and goat cheese in a medium serving bowl.

(continued on next page)

Maple Vinaigrette: Shake all 5 ingredients together in a jar until well combined. Drizzle salad with vinaigrette.

1 serving: 120 Calories; 4 g Total Fat (2 g Mono, 0 g Poly, 1.5 g Sat); trace Cholesterol; 20 g Carbohydrate; 5 g Fibre; 4 g Protein; 230 mg Sodium

Make-ahead Tip
The beets can be roasted and peeled up to 2 days before serving; store in a sealed container in the refrigerator. The maple vinaigrette can also be prepared up to 2 days before serving; store in a sealed jar in the refrigerator. Assemble salad just before serving.

BRUSSELS SPROUTS WITH BACON AND MUSTARD

Serves 6

Small Brussels sprouts that have been cooked until just tender and bright are delicious, so do not overcook them. Overcooking leads to the strong, unpleasant taste that has given the poor sprouts their undeserved reputation.

4 bacon slices, chopped

1/4 cup (60 mL) thinly sliced green onion

2 Tbsp (30 mL) grainy mustard

2 Tbsp (30 mL) orange juice

1 Tbsp (15 mL) butter

2 lbs (900 g) small Brussels sprouts, stalk ends trimmed

Cook bacon in a small frying pan on medium until golden; drain on paper towel. Drain and discard all but 2 tsp (10 mL) drippings. Add onion and cook on medium for about 3 minutes until softened. Add mustard, orange juice and butter, and stir until butter is melted.

Meanwhile, cook sprouts in steamer in large saucepan over simmering water for 10 to 12 minutes until just tender-crisp and bright green; do not overcook. Drain water from pan and remove steamer. Return sprouts to same pan. Add bacon mixture and toss to coat.

1 serving: 130 Calories; 6 g Total Fat (2 g Mono, 0.5 g Poly, 2.5 g Sat); 10 mg Cholesterol; 15 g Carbohydrate; 6 g Fibre; 7 g Protein; 170 mg Sodium

CREAMY LEMON COLESLAW

Serves 14

This salad is a refreshing change during the festive season, but it would make a nice accompaniment to a barbecue during the warmer months too.

CREAMY LEMON DRESSING

1 cup (250 mL) mayonnaise

1/3 cup (75 mL) lemon juice

3 Tbsp (45 mL) granulated sugar

2 Tbsp (30 mL) Dijon mustard

1 Tbsp (15 mL) finely grated lemon zest

1/4 tsp (1 mL) salt

1/4 tsp (1 mL) pepper

COLESLAW

4 cups (1 L) finely shredded green cabbage

4 cups (1 L) finely shredded red cabbage

1 1/2 cups (375 mL) dark raisins

1 cup (250 mL) sliced almonds, toasted (see p. 8)

1 cup (250 mL) thinly sliced celery

1 cup (250 mL) thinly sliced red onion

Creamy Lemon Dressing: Whisk all 7 ingredients together in a small bowl.

Coleslaw: Toss all 6 ingredients in an extra-large serving bowl. Drizzle with dressing and toss.

1 serving: 240 Calories; 17 g Total Fat (2.5 g Mono, 1 g Poly, 2 g Sat); 5 mg Cholesterol; 22 g Carbohydrate; 3 g Fibre; 3 g Protein; 180 mg Sodium

Make-ahead Tip
Prepare all ingredients a day ahead; store them separately in sealed bags in the refrigerator. The dressing can be made 1 to 2 days ahead; store in a sealed container in the refrigerator. Toss everything together just before serving.

Cauliflower Broccoli Bake with Garlic Crumbs

Serves 10

*The cheese sauce and garlic crumb topping makes
this a veggie side dish that the whole family will enjoy.*

CHEESE SAUCE

2 Tbsp (30 mL) butter

2 Tbsp (30 mL) all-purpose
flour

2 cups (500 mL) milk

1 cup (250 mL) grated white
Cheddar cheese

1 tsp (5 mL) prepared
mustard

1/4 tsp (1 mL) pepper

1/4 tsp (1 mL) ground
nutmeg

GARLIC CRUMBS

1 1/2 Tbsp (25 mL) butter

3 garlic cloves, minced

1 cup (250 mL) fine fresh
bread crumbs (see p. 7)

CAULIFLOWER
AND BROCCOLI

1 1/2 lbs (680 g) cauliflower
florets

1 lb (454 g) broccoli florets

Cheese Sauce: Melt butter in a medium saucepan on medium. Add flour and stir until mixture is bubbling. Slowly stir in milk and continue to stir until mixture is smooth. Simmer for about 5 minutes, stirring constantly, until thickened and boiling. Remove from heat. Add remaining 4 ingredients and stir until well combined.

Garlic Crumbs: Melt butter in a medium frying pan on medium. Add garlic and cook for 1 to 2 minutes until garlic is softened and fragrant. Stir in bread crumbs and cook for about 5 minutes until golden brown.

Cauliflower and Broccoli: Preheat oven to 350°F (175°C). Grease a 6 to 8 cup (1.5 to 2 L) baking dish. Cook cauliflower and broccoli in a steamer in a large saucepan over simmering water until bright and tender. Place in prepared dish. Pour cheese sauce over cauliflower and broccoli. Sprinkle bread crumbs over cheese sauce. Bake in preheated oven for about 20 minutes until bubbling and hot.

1 serving: *190 Calories; 9 g Total Fat (1 g Mono, 0 g Poly, 5 g Sat); 25 mg Cholesterol; 20 g Carbohydrate; 2 g Fibre; 9 g Protein; 300 mg Sodium*

Make-ahead Tip

Cheese sauce can be made a day ahead; store in a sealed container in refrigerator. Let stand at room temperature for 30 minutes before using.

CORN BAKE

Serves 10

This recipe is so quick and easy to prepare. Everything is mixed in a bowl and spread into the prepared dish. It is also delicious served cold the next day on sandwiches or toast. Cornflake crumbs are available in packages in grocery stores. You can use fine dry bread crumbs instead if you prefer.

2 x 14 oz (398 mL) cans kernel corn, drained

2 x 14 oz (398 mL) cans creamed corn

2 large eggs

1 cup (250 mL) sour cream

2/3 cup (150 mL) cornflake crumbs

1/2 tsp (2 mL) salt

1/2 tsp (2 mL) pepper

Preheat oven to 350°F (175°C). Grease a 6 to 8 cup (1.5 to 2 L) baking dish. Combine all 7 ingredients in a large bowl. Scrape into prepared baking dish; smooth top. Bake, uncovered, in preheated oven for about 50 minutes until set and top is golden.

(continued on next page)

*1 serving: 190 Calories; 4.5 g Total Fat
(1 g Mono, 0 g Poly, 2 g Sat); 35 mg Cholesterol;
32 g Carbohydrate; 2 g Fibre; 5 g Protein;
630 mg Sodium*

Make-ahead Tip
The corn bake can be prepared 1 to
3 hours ahead; store, covered, in the
refrigerator. Remove from refrigerator
1 hour before baking.

GRAPEFRUIT, FENNEL AND HAZELNUT SALAD

Serves 10

This fresh, lively salad features a mix of flavours that are sure to delight your guests.

BALSAMIC VINAIGRETTE

1/4 cup (60 mL) olive oil

2 Tbsp (30 mL) lemon juice

1 1/2 Tbsp (25 mL) balsamic vinegar

1 Tbsp (15 mL) liquid honey

1/4 tsp (1 mL) salt

1/4 tsp (1 mL) pepper

SALAD

2 red grapefruits

4 cups (1 L) loosely packed mixed baby lettuce leaves

1 medium fennel bulb (white part only), thinly sliced

3 oz (85 g) blue cheese, coarsely crumbled or chopped

1/2 cup (125 mL) hazelnuts (filberts), toasted (see p. 8) and coarsely chopped

Balsamic Vinaigrette: Shake all 6 ingredients together in a jar until well combined.

Salad: Cut both ends from each grapefruit. Place a cut end down on cutting board, and using a small sharp knife, cut down and around fruit, removing rind and as much of the white pith as possible. Place fruit on its side and cut down between membranes of each segment. Repeat with remaining grapefruit. Gently toss grapefruit and remaining 4 ingredients in a large serving bowl. Drizzle with balsamic vinaigrette.

1 serving: 160 Calories; 12 g Total Fat (8 g Mono, 1 g Poly, 2.5 g Sat); 5 mg Cholesterol; 11 g Carbohydrate; 2 g Fibre; 4 g Protein; 190 mg Sodium

Make-ahead Tip

The vinaigrette can be made a day ahead; store in a jar in the refrigerator. The remaining salad ingredients can be prepared a day ahead; store ingredients in sealed plastic bags in the refrigerator.

MUSHROOM PILAF

Serves 8

A pilaf is easy to make—you simply add the ingredients to rice and cook until the liquid is absorbed and the rice is tender. Use any assortment of mushrooms you wish. Basmati rice gives the pilaf a distinct flavour. It is available in the same section as other rice in grocery stores.

2 Tbsp (30 mL) butter
4 cups (1 L) sliced mushrooms

1 Tbsp (15 mL) butter
1 cup (250 mL) finely chopped onion

1 1/2 cups (375 mL) basmati rice
3 cups (750 mL) chicken (or vegetable) broth
3 Tbsp (45 mL) chopped fresh parsley
1 1/2 Tbsp (25 mL) lemon juice
1/4 tsp (1 mL) salt
1/4 tsp (1 mL) pepper

Melt first amount of butter in a large saucepan on medium-high. Add mushrooms and cook for about 5 minutes until mushrooms are softened. Remove from pan and set aside.

Melt second amount of butter in same pan on medium. Add onion and cook for about 5 minutes until softened.

Add rice and stir until coated. Stir in chicken broth. Cover and bring to boil. Turn heat to low and cook, covered, for about 15 minutes until rice is tender. Stir in remaining 4 ingredients. Let stand, covered, for 5 minutes; fluff with fork.

1 serving: 180 Calories; 6 g Total Fat (1 g Mono, 0 g Poly, 3 g Sat); 10 mg Cholesterol; 30 g Carbohydrate; 2 g Fibre; 4 g Protein; 320 mg Sodium

ROASTED CARAMELIZED ONIONS

Serves 12

Onions are added to most savoury dishes, but they also make a delicious side dish on their own. As they cook, they soften and sweeten. Add any leftovers to pasta dishes, stews or casseroles.

6 medium onions

1 Tbsp (15 mL) balsamic vinegar

1 Tbsp (15 mL) canola oil

1/4 tsp (1 mL) salt

1/4 tsp (1 mL) pepper

2 Tbsp (30 mL) brown sugar, packed

Preheat oven to 350°F (175°C). Lightly grease a baking sheet. Peel and quarter onions but do not remove the stalk ends—they help the wedges hold together as the onions cook. Place in large bowl. Add next 4 ingredients and toss to coat. Place on prepared baking sheet. Bake, uncovered, in preheated oven for 50 minutes.

Sprinkle with brown sugar and toss. Bake for 10 to 15 minutes until browned and glazed.

1 serving: 60 Calories; 1 g Total Fat (0.5 g Mono, 0 g Poly, 0 g Sat); 0 mg Cholesterol; 13 g Carbohydrate; 1 g Fibre; trace Protein; 55 mg Sodium

ORANGE SALAD WITH PINE NUT VINAIGRETTE

Serves 8

The Valencia salad from Spain was the inspiration for this recipe. Choose heavy, juicy oranges such as navel or Valencia for best results.

PINE NUT VINAIGRETTE

3 Tbsp (45 mL) pine nuts, toasted (see p. 8) and finely chopped

2 Tbsp (30 mL) olive oil

1 Tbsp (15 mL) red wine vinegar

1 Tbsp (15 mL) liquid honey

pinch of salt

ORANGE SALAD

6 medium oranges

1/4 cup (60 mL) sliced small pitted black olives

1/4 cup (60 mL) thinly sliced green onions

3 Tbsp (45 mL) chopped fresh mint leaves

Pine Nut Vinaigrette: Shake all 5 ingredients together in a small jar until well combined.

Orange Salad: Cut ends from each orange. Place 1 orange, cut-end down, on cutting board. Using a small, sharp knife, cut down and around orange to remove rind and as much of the white pith as possible. Cut orange into 1 inch (2.5 cm) pieces and place in a medium serving bowl. Repeat with remaining oranges.

Add remaining 3 ingredients. Drizzle with pine nut vinaigrette and gently toss.

1 serving: 110 Calories; 6 g Total Fat (3.5 g Mono, 1.5 g Poly, 0.5 g Sat); 0 mg Cholesterol; 13 g Carbohydrate; 2 g Fibre; 1 g Protein; 35 mg Sodium

Make-ahead Tip

The oranges can be prepared a day ahead; store in a sealed container in the refrigerator. The dressing, excluding pine nuts, can be made 1 to 2 days ahead; store in a jar in a cool place. Add pine nuts just before serving.

SMOKED CHEESE MASHED POTATOES

Serves 10

Enjoy a slight twist on regular mashed potatoes. Smoked cheese can be found in grocery and specialty food stores. We used applewood smoked cheese in this recipe.

4 lbs (1.8 kg) russet potatoes, peeled and quartered

1/4 cup (60 mL) butter

1/4 cup (60 mL) milk

2 Tbsp (30 mL) sour cream

1 1/2 cups (375 mL) grated smoked cheese

1/2 tsp (2 mL) salt

1/4 tsp (1 mL) pepper

Cook potatoes in boiling salted water in a large saucepan for 20 to 25 minutes until tender but not mushy. Drain well and return to same pan. Mash until no large lumps remain.

Add butter, milk and sour cream and stir vigorously with a fork until smooth.

Add remaining 3 ingredients and stir until well combined.

1 serving: 250 Calories; 10 g Total Fat (1.5 g Mono, 0 g Poly, 6 g Sat); 25 mg Cholesterol; 42 g Carbohydrate; 3 g Fibre; 8 g Protein; 250 mg Sodium

SCALLOPED POTATOES

Serves 10

This dish is best prepared just before baking. Do not slice the potatoes ahead of time and leave them in water, because doing so prevents them from absorbing the broth and cream as they cook. A mandoline works very well for evenly slicing the potatoes.

4 lbs (1.8 kg) red potatoes, peeled and thinly sliced

10 bacon slices, coarsely chopped, cooked until golden

1 1/2 cups (375 mL) grated white Cheddar cheese

1/2 tsp (2 mL) salt

1/4 tsp (1 mL) pepper

1/4 to 1/2 tsp (1 to 2 mL) ground nutmeg

(continued on next page)

Preheat oven to 350°F (175°C). Grease a shallow 8 cup (2 L) baking dish. Layer potatoes in prepared dish. Scatter bacon and cheese over potatoes. Sprinkle with salt, pepper and nutmeg.

Combine whipping cream and chicken broth in medium bowl and pour over potatoes. Bake, uncovered, in preheated oven for about 1 hour until potatoes are tender and top is golden brown. Cover and let stand for 10 minutes before serving to allow liquid to settle.

1 1/2 cups (375 mL) whipping cream

1 cup (250 mL) chicken broth

1 serving: 360 Calories; 21 g Total Fat (6 g Mono, 1 g Poly, 12 g Sat); 70 mg Cholesterol; 33 g Carbohydrate; 3 g Fibre; 12 g Protein; 380 mg Sodium

ROASTED POTATO SALAD

Serves 8

This recipe is delicious served hot or cold. It also goes great with barbecued meat and chicken.

4 lbs (1.8 kg) small new potatoes, halved

2 Tbsp (30 mL) canola oil

1/2 tsp (2 mL) salt

1/4 tsp (1 mL) pepper

4 garlic cloves, unpeeled and bruised (see p. 6)

1/3 cup (75 mL) finely chopped green onion

1/4 cup (60 mL) finely chopped gherkins

1/4 cup (60 mL) mayonnaise

1/4 cup (60 mL) sour cream

2 Tbsp (30 mL) chopped fresh dill

1 Tbsp (15 mL) creamed horseradish

Preheat oven to 400°F (200°C). Grease a baking sheet. Toss first 5 ingredients on prepared baking sheet. Bake, uncovered, in preheated oven for about 1 hour, turning occasionally, until golden brown. Remove garlic cloves.

Combine remaining 6 ingredients in a large bowl. Add hot potatoes and stir to coat. Serve hot or cold.

1 serving: 180 Calories; 10 g Total Fat (2.5 g Mono, 1 g Poly, 1.5 g Sat); 5 mg Cholesterol; 20 g Carbohydrate; 3 g Fibre; 2 g Protein; 770 mg Sodium

Make-ahead Tip

If you are serving the salad cold, it can be made a day ahead; store in a sealed container in the refrigerator. If you are serving it hot, prepare the dressing a day ahead; store in a sealed container in the refrigerator. Remove dressing from refrigerator 1 hour before tossing it with the hot potatoes.

SPINACH, TOFFEE PECAN AND GOAT CHEESE SALAD

Serves 8

Dried cranberries add a seasonal and delicious touch to this elegant salad.

2/3 cup (150 mL) pecans

1/3 cup (75 mL) granulated sugar

2 Tbsp (30 mL) water

9 oz (255 g) bag baby spinach leaves

4 oz (113 g) goat (chèvre) cheese, coarsely crumbled

1/3 cup (75 mL) dried cranberries

MAPLE VINAIGRETTE

1/4 cup (60 mL) olive oil

2 Tbsp (30 mL) maple syrup

2 Tbsp (30 mL) red wine vinegar

1 tsp (5 mL) grainy mustard

pinch of salt

Preheat oven to 350°F (175°C). Line a baking sheet with parchment paper. Place pecans on prepared baking sheet. Toast in preheated oven for 10 minutes. Remove from oven. Set pan aside, leaving pecans on pan.

Meanwhile, stir sugar and water in a small saucepan on medium until sugar is dissolved. Boil gently for about 5 minutes, without stirring, until mixture is a deep golden colour. Drizzle syrup mixture over pecans. Let stand for about 20 minutes until cooled completely and brittle; coarsely chop.

Toss toffee pecans, spinach, cheese and cranberries in a large serving bowl.

Maple Vinaigrette: Shake all 5 ingredients in a jar until well combined. Drizzle salad with maple vinaigrette.

1 serving: 220 Calories; 16 g Total Fat (9 g Mono, 2.5 g Poly, 3.5 g Sat); 5 mg Cholesterol; 17 g Carbohydrate; 2 g Fibre; 4 g Protein; 85 mg Sodium

Make-ahead Tip
The toffee pecans can be made a week ahead; store in a sealed container. The maple vinaigrette can be made 3 days ahead; store in the refrigerator.

Roasted Sweet Potatoes

Serves 8

These delicious sweet potatoes can be drizzled with honey instead of maple syrup if you prefer.

3 lbs (1.4 kg) orange-fleshed sweet potatoes, peeled and cut into 1 inch (2.5 cm) cubes

2 Tbsp (30 mL) coarsely chopped fresh rosemary

2 Tbsp (30 mL) olive oil

1/2 tsp (2 mL) salt

1/2 tsp (2 mL) pepper

1/4 tsp (1 mL) ground cinnamon

2 Tbsp (30 mL) maple syrup

Preheat oven to 350°F (175°C). Line a baking sheet with parchment paper. Combine first 6 ingredients in a large bowl. Toss to coat sweet potatoes completely with mixture. Arrange in a single layer on prepared baking sheet. Bake for 40 minutes in preheated oven, stirring once during cooking.

Drizzle with maple syrup and toss gently to coat. Bake for about 15 minutes until glazed and lightly browned.

1 serving: 190 Calories; 3.5 g Total Fat (2.5 g Mono, 0 g Poly, 0.5 g Sat); 0 mg Cholesterol; 37 g Carbohydrate; 5 g Fibre; 3 g Protein; 240 mg Sodium

ORANGE MASHED SWEET POTATOES

Serves 10

Orange zest adds a noticeable touch of flavour to this orange-coloured side dish.

1 Tbsp (15 mL) olive oil

1 cup (250 mL) finely chopped onion

1 tsp (5 mL) ground cumin

1/2 tsp (2 mL) pepper

4 lbs (1.8 kg) orange-fleshed sweet potatoes, peeled and cut into large pieces

2 1/2 cups (625 mL) chicken (or vegetable) broth

1/2 tsp (2 mL) salt

1 cup (250 mL) finely grated Parmesan cheese

2 to 3 Tbsp (30 to 45 mL) sour cream

1 to 2 tsp (5 to 10 mL) finely grated orange zest

Heat olive oil in a large pot or Dutch oven on medium. Add onion and cook for about 5 minutes until softened. Add cumin and pepper, and cook for about 1 minute until fragrant.

Stir in sweet potatoes, chicken broth and salt. Cover and bring to a boil on medium-high. Boil for about 15 minutes until tender but not mushy. Drain well and return to same pan. Mash until no large lumps remain.

Add remaining 3 ingredients and stir vigorously with a fork until well combined and smooth.

1 serving: 230 Calories; 4.5 g Total Fat (2 g Mono, 0 g Poly, 2 g Sat); 10 mg Cholesterol; 40 g Carbohydrate; 6 g Fibre; 7 g Protein; 510 mg Sodium

VANILLA CITRUS SALAD

Serves 6

Vanilla beans are available from grocery and specialty food stores. The visible black specks in the salad are the tiny seeds from the pod.

1/2 cup (125 mL) granulated sugar

1/4 cup (60 mL) water

1 vanilla bean, split lengthwise

6 oranges

6 red grapefruits

1/4 cup (60 mL) orange-flavoured liqueur (such as Cointreau)

Stir sugar and water in a small saucepan on medium until sugar is dissolved. Boil gently for 2 minutes, without stirring. Remove from heat. Scrape seeds from vanilla bean into pan and add pod; cool. Pour into large bowl.

Cut both ends from each orange and grapefruit. Place a cut end down on cutting board, and, using a small sharp knife, cut down and around fruit, removing rind and as much of the white pith as possible. Place fruit on its side and cut down between membranes of each segment. Repeat with remaining oranges and grapefruits. Add segmented oranges, grapefruits and liqueur to bowl. Stir and cover. Refrigerate for 6 hours or overnight. Remove vanilla bean just before serving.

***1 serving:** 260 Calories; 0.5 g Total Fat (0 g Mono, 0 g Poly, 0 g Sat); 0 mg Cholesterol; 63 g Carbohydrate; 8 g Fibre; 3 g Protein; 0 mg Sodium*

Make-ahead Tip
The salad is best when made a day ahead of serving to allow flavours to develop. It can be made 2 days ahead; store in a sealed container in the refrigerator.

WILD RICE MEDLEY

Serves 6

Enjoy the natural nuttiness of wild rice enhanced with vegetables, bacon and a little Asian accent. A show-stopping side dish for roasted or braised meats.

2 cups (500 mL) water
1/8 tsp (0.5 mL) salt
2/3 cup (150 mL) wild rice

4 bacon slices, chopped

2 cups (500 mL) chopped fresh white mushrooms
1 cup (250 mL) chopped onion
1 cup (250 mL) diced carrot
1 cup (250 mL) diced celery
2 Tbsp (30 mL) hoisin sauce
1 Tbsp (15 mL) finely grated ginger root (or 3/4 tsp, 4 mL, ground ginger)
1 Tbsp (15 mL) soy sauce
pinch of dried crushed chilies

1/4 cup (60 mL) raw pumpkin seeds, toasted (see p. 8)

Combine water and salt in a small saucepan. Bring to a boil. Add rice. Stir. Reduce heat to medium-low. Simmer, covered, for about 70 minutes, without stirring, until rice is tender. Drain any remaining liquid.

Cook bacon in a large frying pan on medium until crisp. Transfer with slotted spoon to paper towel–lined plate to drain. Drain and discard all but 1 Tbsp (15 mL) drippings.

Add next 8 ingredients. Cook on medium-high for about 7 minutes, stirring often, until carrot is tender-crisp and liquid is almost evaporated. Add rice. Heat and stir for 1 minute. Transfer to serving bowl.

Sprinkle with pumpkin seeds and bacon.

1 serving: *235 Calories; 9.4 g Total Fat (2.2 g Mono, 0.8 g Poly, 2.4 g Sat); 8 mg Cholesterol; 31 g Carbohydrate; 9 g Fibre; 9 g Protein; 702 mg Sodium*

Salmon and Asparagus Crêpes

Makes 8

These crêpes are a welcome addition to any brunch menu.
Serve with the Cranberry Brie Muffins on page 122.

CRÊPES

1 3/4 cups (425 mL) milk

1 1/2 cups (375 mL)
all-purpose flour

2 eggs

1/4 tsp (1 mL) salt

FILLING

2 Tbsp (30 mL) butter

3/4 cup (175 mL) finely
chopped onion

3 Tbsp (45 mL) all-purpose
flour

1 3/4 cups (425 mL) milk

1 cup (250 mL) grated Swiss
cheese

1/2 cup (125 mL) finely
grated Parmesan cheese

4 oz (113 g) smoked salmon,
coarsely chopped

2 Tbsp (30 mL) sour cream

1 Tbsp (15 mL) lemon juice

salt and pepper, to taste

1 lb (454 g) asparagus,
trimmed and halved
lengthwise if thick

Crêpes: Heat an 8 inch (20 cm) non-stick frying pan on medium-high and grease with butter or spray with cooking spray. Whisk all 4 ingredients in a medium bowl until smooth. Add 1/3 cup (75 mL) batter to pan, swirling pan to ensure batter spreads evenly. Cook for about 1 minute until golden underneath; flip. Cook for about 1 minute until golden on bottom. Stack crêpes on a plate and cover with foil as you cook them.

Filling: Melt butter in a medium saucepan on medium. Add onion and cook for about 5 minutes until softened. Add flour and cook for about 1 minute. Slowly stir in milk and cook for about 5 minutes, stirring constantly, until sauce is thickened and boiling; remove from heat.

Stir in next 6 ingredients. Cover and keep warm.

(continued on next page)

Meanwhile, cook asparagus in a steamer in a large saucepan over simmering water for about 2 minutes until bright green and crisp; do not overcook. Lay 1 crêpe on a cutting board. Spoon about 1/2 cup (125 mL) salmon filling down centre of crêpe. Lay 3 to 5 asparagus on filling. Roll up crêpe to enclose filling. Repeat with remaining crêpes, filling and asparagus.

1 crêpe: 310 Calories; 12 g Total Fat (3 g Mono, 1 g Poly, 7 g Sat); 70 mg Cholesterol; 31 g Carbohydrate; 2 g Fibre; 19 g Protein; 410 mg Sodium

Make-ahead Tip

Crêpes can be made 2 days ahead; store on a plate, wrapped in plastic wrap, in the refrigerator. Heat on low power for 30 to 60 seconds in the microwave until warm.

BACON AND HERB BREAKFAST BAKE

Serves 8

*Serve this dish warm and drizzled with maple syrup.
It needs to be prepared a day ahead of baking.*

8 bacon slices, chopped

2 tsp (10 mL) canola oil

1 cup (250 mL) chopped
onion

1 cup (250 mL) chopped
red pepper

10 bread slices, cut into
1 inch (2.5 cm) cubes

8 large eggs

4 cups (1 L) milk

1/4 cup (60 mL) mayonnaise

3 Tbsp (45 mL) chopped
fresh parsley

3 Tbsp (45 mL) Dijon
mustard

2 Tbsp (30 mL) chopped
fresh chives

1/4 tsp (1 mL) salt

1/4 tsp (1 mL) pepper

Lightly grease a 10 to 12 cup (2.5 to 3 L) baking dish that has 3 to 3 1/2 inch (7.5 to 9 cm) sides. Cook bacon in a large frying pan on medium until golden brown. Transfer to paper towel. Discard bacon fat. Heat oil in same pan on medium, and add onion, red pepper and bacon. Cook for about 5 minutes until onion is softened. Place bread in prepared baking dish. Scatter onion mixture over bread.

Whisk remaining 8 ingredients in a large bowl; pour over bread. Cover and refrigerate for 8 hours or overnight. Let stand at room temperature for 1 hour before baking. Cook in a 350°F (175°C) oven for about 1 hour until set and golden brown.

1 serving: 390 Calories; 18 g Total Fat
(4.5 g Mono, 2.5 g Poly, 4.5 g Sat);
155 mg Cholesterol; 38 g Carbohydrate;
2 g Fibre; 18 g Protein; 580 mg Sodium

Freezer Almond Cranberry Buns

Makes 12 buns

Fill your kitchen with the aroma of freshly baked sticky buns! You'll love this recipe, not only for Christmas but for anytime company's expected. You can keep these buns, unbaked, in the freezer for up to one month. They'll need to thaw in the refrigerator overnight before baking.

1/2 cup (125 mL) milk

1/4 cup (60 mL) granulated sugar

2 Tbsp (30 mL) butter (or hard margarine)

1/4 tsp (1 mL) salt

1 cup (250 mL) warm water

2 1/2 cups (625 mL) all-purpose flour

1/4 oz (8 g) envelope of instant yeast (or 2 1/4 tsp, 11 mL)

1/4 tsp (1 mL) ground nutmeg

3/4 cup (175 mL) all-purpose flour

ALMOND FILLING

1/3 cup (75 mL) butter (or hard margarine), softened

1/3 cup (75 mL) brown sugar, packed

1/3 cup (75 mL) ground almonds

2 Tbsp (30 mL) all-purpose flour

1 large egg, fork-beaten

2 tsp (10 mL) almond extract

(continued on next page)

Combine milk, sugar, butter and salt in a small saucepan. Heat and stir on medium until butter is melted and sugar is dissolved. Remove from heat. Add warm water (see p. 8). Stir. Set aside.

Combine first amount of flour, yeast and nutmeg in a large bowl. Make a well in centre. Add milk mixture. Stir well.

Add second amount of flour, 1/4 cup (60 mL) at a time, mixing well after each addition until a soft dough forms. Turn out onto lightly floured surface. Knead for 5 to 10 minutes, adding extra flour 1 Tbsp (15 mL) at a time if necessary to prevent sticking, until smooth and elastic. Place in a separate greased large bowl, turning once to grease top. Cover with greased waxed paper and tea towel. Let stand in oven with light on and door closed for 30 minutes. Punch down dough. Turn out onto lightly floured surface. Knead for about 1 minute until smooth. Roll out to 9 x 14 inch (23 x 35 cm) rectangle.

Almond Filling: Beat first 4 ingredients in a medium bowl until well combined. Add egg and extract. Beat until smooth. Makes about 1 cup (250 mL) filling. Spread filling on dough rectangle, leaving 1 inch (2.5 cm) edge on 1 long side.

Sprinkle cranberries and slivered almonds over filling. Press down lightly. Roll up from covered long side, jelly-roll style. Press seam against roll to seal.

Maple Glaze: Measure butter, brown sugar and maple syrup into microwave-safe medium bowl. Microwave, covered, on high (100%) for about 45 seconds until butter is melted. Stir well. Makes about 1/2 cup (125 mL) glaze. Spread glaze in greased and parchment paper–lined 9 x 13 inch (23 x 33 cm) pan (see Note). Cut roll into

12 equal slices using floured knife. Arrange, cut-side up, on top of glaze in pan. Cover tightly with greased plastic wrap and foil. Freeze immediately. When ready to thaw, remove foil and plastic wrap. Cover loosely with greased plastic wrap. Thaw in refrigerator for at least 8 hours or overnight. Let stand at room temperature for 1 hour. Bake, uncovered, in 350°F (175°C) oven for about 40 minutes until golden. Let stand in pan for 5 minutes before inverting onto serving platter. Makes 12 buns.

1 bun: 395 Calories; 17.5 g Total Fat (6.8 g Mono, 1.7 g Poly, 7.9 g Sat); 49 mg Cholesterol; 54 g Carbohydrate; 3 g Fibre; 7 g Protein; 183 mg Sodium

Note: Greasing the bottom and sides of the pan will help secure the parchment paper. Extend the parchment paper over both long sides for easy removal.

1 cup (250 mL) dried cranberries

2/3 cup (150 mL) slivered almonds

MAPLE GLAZE

1/4 cup (60 mL) butter (or hard margarine)

1/4 cup (60 mL) brown sugar, packed

2 Tbsp (30 mL) maple (or maple-flavoured syrup)

CRANBERRY BRIE MUFFINS

Makes 12

These muffins can also be made in mini muffin pans and served as an appetizer with a cheese and fruit platter. If you do use mini muffin pans, decrease the cooking time by about 10 minutes. These muffins are best served warm, fresh from the oven.

2 1/3 cups (575 mL) all-purpose flour

3 Tbsp (45 mL) brown sugar, packed

4 tsp (20 mL) baking powder

1/4 tsp (1 mL) salt

1/2 cup (125 mL) dried cranberries

5 oz (140 g) brie cheese, chopped

1 large egg

1 cup (250 mL) milk

1/3 cup (75 mL) canola oil

1/3 cup (75 mL) cranberry jelly

Preheat oven to 375°F (190°C). Line a 12-cup muffin pan with muffin liners and spray with cooking spray. Sift first 4 ingredients into a large bowl. Add cranberries and cheese and stir.

Whisk remaining 4 ingredients in a medium bowl and add to flour mixture. Stir until just combined; do not overmix. Spoon mixture into prepared muffin pan, filling each cup to three-quarters full. Bake in preheated oven for 20 to 25 minutes until a toothpick inserted into centre of muffin comes out clean.

1 muffin: 240 Calories; 10 g Total Fat (4.5 g Mono, 2 g Poly, 3 g Sat); 25 mg Cholesterol; 30 g Carbohydrate; trace Fibre; 6 g Protein; 240 mg Sodium

Make-ahead Tip
These can be made 1 day ahead; warm for 20 seconds each in the microwave.

WALNUT AND DATE LOAVES

Makes 9

These mini loaves make a lovely addition to a festive gift basket. For extra decadence, slice and serve with butter.

1 1/2 cups (375 mL) pitted dates, chopped

1 cup (250 mL) brown sugar, packed

1 cup (250 mL) water

1/3 cup (75 mL) butter

1 large egg, fork-beaten

2 cups (500 mL) all-purpose flour

4 tsp (20 mL) baking powder

1/2 tsp (2 mL) baking soda

1/4 tsp (1 mL) salt

2/3 cup (150 mL) walnuts, toasted (see p. 8) and coarsely chopped

icing sugar, for dusting (optional)

Preheat oven to 350°F (175°C). Grease nine 2 1/2 x 4 x 1 inch (6.5 x 10 x 2.5 cm) mini loaf pans. Combine first 4 ingredients in a medium saucepan on medium until butter melts and sugar dissolves. Bring to a boil, then remove from heat; let cool. Add egg and stir until well combined.

Sift next 4 ingredients into date mixture. Add walnuts and stir until well combined.

Spoon mixture into prepared pans until three-quarters full. Bake in preheated oven for about 30 minutes until wooden pick inserted into centre of loaf comes out clean. Let stand in pans for 10 minutes before transferring to wire rack to cool. Dust with icing sugar if desired. Best served fresh and still warm from the oven.

1 serving: 400 Calories; 13 g Total Fat (2.5 g Mono, 4.5 g Poly, 5 g Sat); 35 mg Cholesterol; 69 g Carbohydrate; 3 g Fibre; 5 g Protein; 330 mg Sodium

Make-ahead Tip
The loaves can be made 1 month ahead; freeze in sealed bags.

STRAWBERRY BREAD PUDDING

Serves 8

You can use any of your favourite jams for this recipe.

1/2 cup (125 mL) dark raisins

7 x 1/2 inch (12 mm) thick French bread slices

3 Tbsp (45 mL) butter, softened

1/3 cup (75 mL) strawberry jam

4 large eggs

3 cups (750 mL) milk

1/2 cup (125 mL) granulated sugar

2 tsp (10 mL) vanilla extract

Preheat oven to 350°F (175°C). Grease a shallow 6 to 7 cup (1.5 to 1.75 L) baking dish. Scatter 1/4 cup (60 mL) raisins over bottom of prepared dish. Spread bread slices with butter and jam. Arrange bread slices, slightly overlapping, in a single layer over raisins in dish. Sprinkle with remaining raisins.

Whisk remaining 4 ingredients in a large bowl. Pour over bread and let stand for 15 minutes. Place baking dish in a roasting pan and pour enough hot water into roasting pan to come halfway up sides of baking dish. Bake in preheated oven for about 1 hour until centre is set. Let stand for 15 minutes before serving.

1 serving: 280 Calories; 7 g Total Fat (2 g Mono, 0 g Poly, 4 g Sat); 85 mg Cholesterol; 84 g Carbohydrate; trace Fibre; 8 g Protein; 220 mg Sodium

Make-ahead Tip

This recipe can be made 2 days ahead. Serve cold or cover with foil and reheat in 325°F (160°C) oven for 15 to 20 minutes.

CINNAMON SCROLLS

Makes 18

These rolls are best served warm, although they can be made a day ahead and reheated in the microwave for about 20 seconds each. When making dough, it is always best to start with a little less flour and add more as needed.

CINNAMON FILLING

1/2 cup (125 mL) butter, softened

1/2 cup (125 mL) brown sugar, packed

2 tsp (10 mL) ground cinnamon

2/3 cup (150 mL) ground almonds

DOUGH

2/3 cup (150 mL) warm milk

2 tsp (10 mL) active dry yeast

2 large eggs, room temperature

1/4 cup (60 mL) granulated sugar

2 1/2 to 3 cups (625 to 750 mL) all-purpose flour

1/2 tsp (2 mL) salt

1/3 cup (75 mL) butter, melted

Cinnamon Filling: Combine all 4 ingredients in a small bowl until well mixed.

Dough: Lightly grease muffin pans (18 muffin cups are needed). Whisk first 4 ingredients in a medium bowl until well combined.

Combine flour and salt in a large bowl; make a well in centre. Add milk mixture and butter, and stir until mixture forms a soft dough. Turn onto a lightly floured surface and knead for 5 to 10 minutes until smooth and elastic. Place dough in a lightly greased bowl; turn to coat. Cover with greased plastic wrap and a tea towel and let stand in a warm place for about 1 1/2 hours until dough is doubled in size. Roll out dough on a lightly floured surface to 18 x 10 inch (45 x 25 cm) rectangle, with a long side closest to you. Spread filling evenly over dough, leaving a 1 inch (2.5 cm) border along top long side. Starting with long side closest to you, roll up dough to enclose filling. Cut into eighteen 1 inch (2.5 cm) pieces. Place each piece, cut-side up, in muffin pans. Cover with greased plastic wrap and tea towel, and let stand in warm place for 45 minutes until risen.

Preheat oven to 350°F (175°C). Bake on centre rack for 20 to 25 minutes until golden brown.

1 scroll: 200 Calories; 11 g Total Fat (3.5 g Mono, 1 g Poly, 6 g Sat); 40 mg Cholesterol; 24 g Carbohydrate; 1 g Fibre; 4 g Protein; 140 mg Sodium

CHRISTMAS PUDDING WITH TWO SAUCES

Serves 8

This delicious pudding is steamed. Pudding steamers can be found in kitchen specialty stores.

1 cup (250 mL) brown
sugar, packed

1 cup (250 mL) dark raisins

1 cup (250 mL) golden
raisins

1 cup (250 mL) pitted dates,
chopped

1 cup (250 mL) pitted
prunes, chopped

1 cup (250 mL) water

1/2 cup (125 mL) butter

1/2 cup (125 mL) mixed peel

1 tsp (5 mL) baking soda

2 large eggs, fork-beaten

2 cups (500 mL) all-purpose
flour

2 tsp (10 mL) baking
powder

1/2 tsp (2 mL) ground
cinnamon

1/2 tsp (2 mL) ground
nutmeg

1/4 tsp (1 mL) ground
cloves

(continued on next page)

Grease an 8 cup (2 L) pudding steamer and line base with parchment paper. Combine first 8 ingredients in a large saucepan. Stir on medium until sugar dissolves and butter melts. Bring to a boil, then reduce heat to medium-low. Simmer, uncovered, for 7 minutes. Remove from heat and immediately stir in baking soda; cool.

Add eggs and stir until well combined.

Sift next 5 ingredients into pudding mixture and stir until well combined. Spoon into prepared pudding steamer and smooth top. Cover steamer with parchment paper and then foil, allowing parchment paper and foil to come 1 to 2 inches (2.5 to 5 cm) over edge. Tie string around rim of steamer, securing paper and foil. Place small heat-resistant plate on bottom of a pot. Place steamer on plate. Add enough boiling water to come halfway up side of steamer. Cover pot with a tight-fitting lid. Boil for 5 hours, adding more water when necessary. Let stand for 20 minutes before turning out. Cuts into 8 wedges. Serve warm with hard sauce and warm brandy sauce.

Hard Sauce: Beat icing sugar and butter in a small bowl with an electric mixer for 5 to 10 minutes until light and fluffy. Add liqueur and zest, and beat until well combined. Spoon into a 2 cup (500 mL) serving dish, cover; chill until set.

Warm Brandy Sauce: Stir sugar and water in a small saucepan on medium until sugar dissolves. Boil gently, without stirring, for about 5 minutes until mixture turns a pale golden. Stir in whipping cream carefully—use caution because mixture may bubble up. Add brandy and stir until mixture is hot but not boiling. Remove from heat and add butter. Stir until melted. Serve warm.

1 serving: 1090 Calories; 43 g Total Fat (12 g Mono, 2 g Poly, 27 g Sat); 150 mg Cholesterol; 166 g Carbohydrate; 7 g Fibre; 7 g Protein; 540 mg Sodium

Make-ahead Tip

The pudding can be made 1 month ahead; wrap in plastic wrap and foil and store in the refrigerator. To reheat pudding, cut into wedges, cover and microwave on 100% power for 30 seconds until warm. Or place whole pudding into a greased pudding steamer, cover with tight-fitting lid or foil and boil for 1 hour until hot.

HARD SAUCE

1 3/4 cups (425 mL) icing (confectioner's) sugar

1 cup (250 mL) butter, softened

1/4 cup (60 mL) orange-flavoured liqueur (such as Cointreau)

1 tsp (5 mL) finely grated orange zest

WARM BRANDY SAUCE

1 cup (250 mL) granulated sugar

1/4 cup (60 mL) water

1/2 cup (125 mL) whipping cream

1/4 cup (60 mL) brandy

2 Tbsp (30 mL) butter

STRAWBERRY CHOCOLATE TRIFLE

Serves 14

For best results, make the trifle a day ahead.

2 x 3 oz (85 g) packages strawberry-flavoured jelly powder

Prepare both packages of gelatin according to package directions; pour into a shallow baking dish and refrigerate for about 3 hours until set. Cut into 1/2 inch (12 mm) cubes.

3/4 cup (175 mL) orange juice

1/2 cup (125 mL) orange-flavoured liqueur (such as Cointreau) or orange juice

2 x 4 oz (125 g) packages ladyfingers

Combine orange juice and liqueur in a small bowl. Dip half of ladyfingers into juice mixture and place over bottom and partway up side of 14 to 16 cup (3.5 to 4 L) trifle dish. Spoon half of jelly cubes over biscuits.

1 1/2 cups (375 mL) whipping cream

1/2 cup (125 mL) strawberry jam, room temperature

Beat first amount whipping cream in a medium bowl until soft peaks form; fold in jam.

1/2 cup (125 mL) whipping cream

7 oz (200 g) dark chocolate, chopped

1/2 cup (125 mL) small white marshmallows

Heat second amount of whipping cream in a medium saucepan on medium-high until bubbling. Remove from heat and stir in first amount of chocolate and marshmallows. Stir until chocolate and marshmallows are melted.

2 baskets strawberries, hulled and sliced

Spoon half of strawberries over jelly cubes. Spread with half of chocolate sauce, then spread with half of whipped cream mixture. Dip remaining ladyfingers in remaining juice mixture and layer over whipped cream mixture. Spoon remaining jelly cubes over biscuits. Spoon remaining strawberries over jelly cubes. Spread remaining chocolate sauce over strawberries and spread with remaining whipped cream mixture. Cover and refrigerate for 8 hours or overnight.

3 1/2 oz (100 g) dark chocolate, coarsely grated

Sprinkle with grated chocolate just before serving.

1 serving: 390 Calories; 20 g Total Fat (4 g Mono, 0.5 g Poly, 11 g Sat); 100 mg Cholesterol; 42 g Carbohydrate; 3 g Fibre; 11 g Protein; 310 mg Sodium

FRUITCAKE

Cuts into about 30 pieces

This dark fruitcake does not contain eggs and is sweetened with condensed milk, making it moist and delicious. The fruit can be soaked in rum 1 month in advance.

2 cups (500 mL) dark raisins

2 cups (500 mL) pitted dates, chopped

1 cup (250 mL) pitted prunes, chopped

1 cup (250 mL) golden raisins

1 cup (250 mL) red glazed cherries, halved

3/4 cup (175 mL) spiced rum

2/3 cup (150 mL) chopped glazed pineapple

1/3 cup (150 mL) mixed peel

1 cup (250 mL) butter, cubed

1 cup (250 mL) water

11 oz (300 mL) can sweetened condensed milk

2 cups (500 mL) all-purpose flour

1 tsp (5 mL) ground ginger

1 tsp (5 mL) baking powder

1 tsp (5 mL) baking soda

1/2 tsp (2 mL) ground cinnamon

1/2 tsp (2 mL) ground nutmeg

1/3 cup (75 mL) pecan halves

12 red glazed cherries, halved

12 green glazed cherries, halved

1/3 cup (75 mL) spiced rum

Line a deep 9 inch (23 cm) round pan with 3 layers of parchment paper, ensuring that paper comes 2 inches (5 cm) up side of pan. Combine first 8 ingredients in a large bowl. Cover and let stand for at least 12 hours, stirring occasionally.

Spoon into a large saucepan and add butter and water. Cook on medium-high, stirring, until butter melts. Simmer, uncovered, for 5 minutes, stirring occasionally. Spoon into an extra-large bowl; cool. Stir in condensed milk.

Preheat oven to 300°F (150°C). Combine next 6 ingredients in a medium bowl. Add to fruit mixture and mix well. Spread mixture into prepared pan; knock bottom of pan on solid surface to remove any air pockets in cake. Smooth top of cake.

Arrange pecans and cherries in decorative pattern over top of cake. Bake in preheated oven for 2 1/2 to 3 hours until firm and a thin-bladed knife inserted into centre of cake comes out clean—the knife may be a little bit sticky from fruit. Cover cake loosely with brown paper or foil during cooking if top is over-browning.

Drizzle second amount of rum over cake. Cover with foil and let cool in pan. To serve, cut cake into 1 inch (2.5 cm) thick slices, then cut each slice into 2 inch (5 cm) wide pieces.

1 piece: 290 Calories; 8 g Total Fat (2.5 g Mono, 0.5 g Poly, 4.5 g Sat); 20 mg Cholesterol; 50 g Carbohydrate; 3 g Fibre; 3 g Protein; 115 mg Sodium

Make-ahead Tip

Wrap cake well in plastic wrap and foil, and store in a sealed container for up to 3 months. It can also be frozen for up to 6 months.

GINGER AND DATE CAKE WITH TOFFEE RUM SAUCE

Serves 8

This decadent, wintery dessert is sure to become a favourite.

1 cup (250 mL) dates, pitted and coarsely chopped

1 cup (250 mL) water

1 tsp (5 mL) baking soda

1 cup (250 mL) brown sugar, packed

2 large eggs

1/3 cup (75 mL) butter, softened

1 1/4 cups (300 mL) all-purpose flour

2 tsp (10 mL) baking powder

1/2 cup (125 mL) crystallized ginger, chopped

TOFFEE RUM SAUCE

1/2 cup (125 mL) brown sugar, packed

1/2 cup (125 mL) butter

1/2 cup (125 mL) whipping cream

1/4 cup (60 mL) spiced rum

Preheat oven to 350°F (175°C). Grease an 8 inch (20 cm) springform pan and line with parchment paper. Combine dates and water in a medium saucepan on medium-high. Bring to a boil, then remove from heat and add baking soda (use caution; mixture will bubble up); cool.

Beat brown sugar, eggs and butter in a medium bowl with an electric mixer until well combined. Sift flour and baking powder into butter mixture. Add date mixture and ginger, and beat until well combined. Scrape mixture into prepared pan. Bake in preheated oven for 55 to 60 minutes until wooden pick inserted in centre comes out clean. Let stand in pan for 10 minutes before transferring to wire rack to cool.

Toffee Rum Sauce: Combine first 3 ingredients in a medium saucepan on medium until sugar dissolves and butter melts. Boil for 3 minutes, without stirring. Remove from heat and stir in rum. Serve cake warm or cold with toffee rum sauce.

Make-ahead Tip
Cake and sauce can be made a day ahead; reheat in microwave until warm.

1 serving: 580 Calories; 25 g Total Fat (7 g Mono, 1 g Poly, 15 g Sat); 100 mg Cholesterol; 86 g Carbohydrate; 2 g Fibre; 4 g Protein; 410 mg Sodium

FIGGY ORANGE CAKE

Cuts into 16 pieces

This buttery spice cake is filled with the appealing texture of figs and is dressed up with a simple glaze. You can also garnish the cake with fresh figs for an unexpected look.

1 cup (250 mL) granulated sugar

1/2 cup (125 mL) brown sugar, packed

1/2 cup (125 mL) butter (or hard margarine), softened

3 large eggs

1 tsp (5 mL) vanilla extract

2 1/2 cups (625 mL) all-purpose flour

1 tsp (5 mL) baking powder

1 tsp (5 mL) baking soda

1/2 tsp (2 mL) ground cinnamon

1/2 tsp (2 mL) ground ginger

1/2 tsp (2 mL) salt

1 1/4 cups (300 mL) orange juice

1 cup (250 mL) chopped dried figs

2 tsp (10 mL) grated orange zest (see p. 8)

1 cup (250 mL) icing (confectioner's) sugar

3 Tbsp (45 mL) orange juice

Preheat oven to 350°F (175°C). Grease and flour a 10 inch (25 cm) angel food tube pan with removable bottom. Beat sugar, brown sugar and butter in a large bowl until light and fluffy. Add eggs, 1 at a time, beating well after each addition. Add vanilla. Stir.

Combine next 6 ingredients in a medium bowl. Add flour mixture to butter mixture in 3 additions, alternating with first amount of orange juice in 2 additions, stirring well after each addition until just combined.

Add figs and orange zest. Stir. Spread evenly in prepared pan. Bake in preheated oven for about 1 hour until wooden pick inserted in centre of cake comes out clean. Let stand in pan on wire rack for 30 minutes. Run knife around edge of pan to loosen cake. Remove bottom of pan with cake. Run knife around bottom and centre tube of pan to loosen cake. Invert cake onto serving plate. Cool.

Stir icing sugar and second amount of orange juice in separate medium bowl until smooth. Drizzle over top of cake, allowing glaze to flow down sides.

1 piece: 265 Calories; 7 g Total Fat (2 g Mono, 0 g Poly, 4 g Sat); 41 mg Cholesterol; 49 g Carbohydrate; 2 g Fibre; 3 g Protein; 210 mg Sodium

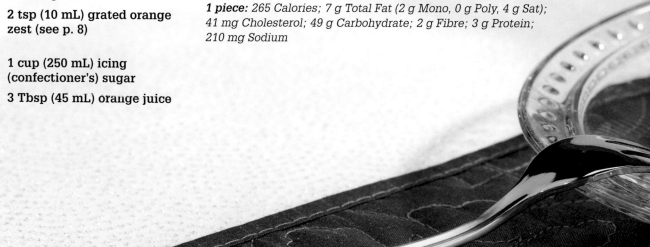

CHOCOLATE DESSERT CAKE

Serves 10

Remove cake from the refrigerator at least 1 hour before serving. This cake is delicious served with ice cream or whipped cream.

10 1/2 oz (300 g) dark chocolate, chopped

1 cup (250 mL) butter

3/4 cup (175 mL) brown sugar, packed

3 Tbsp (45 mL) coffee-flavoured liqueur (such as Kahlúa)

2 Tbsp (30 mL) strong prepared coffee

1 cup (250 mL) all-purpose flour

1/4 cup (60 mL) cocoa powder

1/2 tsp (2 mL) baking powder

2 large eggs, fork-beaten

FUDGE ICING

3 Tbsp (45 mL) butter

2 Tbsp (30 mL) water

1/4 cup (60 mL) granulated sugar

3/4 cup (175 mL) icing (confectioner's) sugar

3 Tbsp (45 mL) cocoa powder

cocoa powder, for dusting

Preheat oven to 325°F (160°C). Grease a 9 inch (23 cm) springform pan and line with parchment paper. Stir first 5 ingredients in a large saucepan on low until chocolate and butter is melted and sugar is dissolved; cool.

Add next 4 ingredients and whisk until well combined and smooth. Pour mixture into prepared pan. Bake in preheated oven for 1 to 1 1/4 hours until wooden pick inserted in centre comes out clean. Let cool in pan.

(continued on next page)

Fudge Icing: Stir butter, water and sugar in a small saucepan on medium until sugar is dissolved. Add icing sugar and cocoa and stir until smooth. Scrape into a small bowl. Cover and refrigerate for about 1 hour until thickened and spreadable.

Remove cooled cake from pan. Spread with fudge icing. Cover and refrigerate for 6 hours or overnight. Dust with cocoa if desired.

1 serving. 500 Calories, 33 g Total Fat (6 g Mono, 1 g Poly, 20 g Sat); 00 mg Cholesterol; 59 g Carbohydrate; 4 g Fibre; 5 g Protein; 190 mg Sodium

Make-ahead Tip
Cake can be made 3 to 5 days ahead; cover and store in the refrigerator.

WHITE CHOCOLATE AND COFFEE CHEESECAKE

Serves 16

A truly decadent dessert flavoured with almond liqueur. This recipe is sure to be a popular addition to any festive feast.

8 oz (250 g) package vanilla-flavoured wafers

1 cup (250 mL) sliced almonds, toasted (see p. 8)

1/2 cup (125 mL) butter, melted

FILLING

1/2 cup (125 mL) cold strong prepared coffee

1/4 oz (7 g) envelope unflavoured gelatin

2 x 8 oz (250 g) packages cream cheese, softened

1/2 cup (125 mL) granulated sugar

1/4 cup (60 mL) almond-flavoured liqueur (such as Amaretto)

14 oz (400 g) white chocolate, melted (see p. 7)

1 cup (250 mL) whipping cream

16 chocolate-coated coffee beans

Grease a 9 inch (23 cm) springform pan and line with parchment paper. Process wafers and almonds in a food processor until mixture resembles fine crumbs. Add butter and process until well combined. Scrape mixture into prepared pan. Using a flat-bottomed, straight-sided glass, press mixture over base and three-quarters up sides of pan. Refrigerate for 30 minutes.

Filling: Place coffee in a small saucepan; sprinkle gelatin over coffee. Stir on low until gelatin dissolves; cool slightly.

With an electric mixer, beat cream cheese, sugar and liqueur in a large bowl until smooth. Add chocolate and gelatin mixture and beat until well combined. Scrape into crust and smooth top. Cover and refrigerate for 8 hours or overnight.

With an electric mixer, beat whipping cream in a small bowl until soft peaks form. Spread whipped cream over cheesecake. Arrange coffee beans around top. Carefully run knife around outer edge of cheesecake before removing ring from pan.

1 serving: 480 Calories; 35 g Total Fat (7 g Mono, 1.5 g Poly, 18 g Sat); 65 mg Cholesterol; 36 g Carbohydrate; 1 g Fibre; 5 g Protein; 200 mg Sodium

Make-ahead Tip
The cheesecake is best made a day ahead, but it can also be made 3 days ahead.

LEMON CURD AND CRANBERRY BAKED CHEESECAKE

Serves 12

This dessert needs to be made a day ahead.

2/3 cup (150 mL) dried cranberries

1/3 cup (75 mL) lemon juice

8 oz (250 g) package vanilla-flavoured wafers

1 cup (250 mL) walnuts

2/3 cup (150 mL) butter, melted

3 large eggs

2/3 cup (150 mL) granulated sugar

2 x 8 oz (250 g) packages cream cheese, softened

2 Tbsp (30 mL) finely grated lemon zest (see p. 8)

LEMON CURD TOPPING

1 cup (250 mL) butter

3/4 cup (175 mL) granulated sugar

2/3 cup (150 mL) lemon juice

3 large eggs

Grease a 9 inch (23 cm) springform pan and line with parchment paper. Combine cranberries and juice in a small bowl and let stand for 30 minutes.

Meanwhile, place wafers and walnuts in a food processor or blender and process until mixture resembles fine crumbs; transfer to a medium bowl. Add butter and stir until well combined. Press mixture into prepared pan using a flat-bottom, straight-sided glass until mixture comes two-thirds up side of pan. Chill for 30 minutes.

Preheat oven to 350°F (175°C). Beat eggs and sugar in a medium bowl with an electric mixer until thick and pale. Add cream cheese, lemon zest and cranberry mixture, and beat until smooth. Pour mixture into crust and smooth top. Place on baking sheet. Bake in preheated oven for 45 to 55 minutes until filling is just set. Mixture will continue to set on cooling. Let cool in oven with door ajar. Filling may separate from crust a little. Cover and refrigerate for about 3 hours until cold.

(contined on next page)

Lemon Curd Topping: Stir butter, sugar and lemon juice on medium until butter melts. Remove from heat and let cool for 10 minutes. Whisk in eggs until well combined. Cook on low, stirring, for about 10 minutes until thickened. Do not overheat mixture or it will curdle. Strain into a small bowl. Discard solids. Cover and refrigerate, stirring occasionally, until cold. Mixture will thicken on cooling. Spread curd evenly over top of cold cheesecake. Cover and refrigerate for 8 hours or overnight. Carefully run a knife around outer edge of cheesecake before removing ring from pan.

1 serving: 660 Calories; 51 g Total Fat (10 g Mono, 6 g Poly, 26 g Sat); 175 mg Cholesterol; 46 g Carbohydrate; 2 g Fibre; 8 g Protein; 380 mg Sodium

Make-ahead Tip

The cheesecake is best made a day ahead; cover and store in the refrigerator. The lemon curd can be made 3 days ahead and kept covered in refrigerator.

CREAM CHEESE TEA RING

Cuts into 14 pieces

This ring is worthy of your finest holiday get-together. A fancy treat, the fluffy biscuit ring contains a surprise filling of fruit, nuts and cream cheese.

8 oz (250 g) package cream cheese, softened

1/4 cup (60 mL) granulated sugar

1/2 tsp (2 mL) vanilla extract

2 cups (500 mL) all-purpose flour

2 Tbsp (30 mL) granulated sugar

4 tsp (20 mL) baking powder

3/4 tsp (4 mL) salt

1/4 cup (60 mL) cold butter (or margarine), cut up

3/4 cup (175 mL) milk, approximately

1/3 cup (75 mL) chopped pecans (or walnuts or almonds)

1/3 cup (75 mL) chopped raisins

1/3 cup (75 mL) chopped red glazed cherries

(continued on next page)

Beat cream cheese, first amount of sugar and vanilla in a small bowl until smooth. Set aside.

Combine next 4 ingredients in a large bowl. Cut in butter until mixture resembles coarse crumbs. Stir, adding milk until a soft dough forms. Turn out onto lightly floured surface. Roll out to 10 x 14 inch (25 x 35 cm) rectangle. Spread with cream cheese mixture, leaving 3/4 inch (2 cm) edge.

Sprinkle pecans, raisins and cherries over cream cheese mixture. Roll up, jelly roll-style, from long side. Press seam against roll to seal. Shape into ring. Place, seam-side down, on greased baking sheet. Pinch ends together to seal. Cut ring 14 times from outside edge to within 1 inch (2.5 cm) of centre using scissors. Turn each wedge on its side, all in the same direction, allowing them to overlap. Bake minutes until golden brown. Let stand on baking sheet on wire rack for about 30 minutes until cool.

Almond Glaze: Combine icing sugar and almond extract in small bowl. Stir, adding enough milk until a smooth, barely pourable consistency. Makes about 1/4 cup (60 mL) glaze. Drizzle or pipe over tea ring.

Sprinkle with pecans.

1 serving: 229 Calories; 11.1 g Total Fat (3.6 g Mono, 0.9 g Poly, 5.9 g Sat); 27 mg Cholesterol; 29 g Carbohydrate; 1 g Fibre; 4 g Protein; 281 mg Sodium

ALMOND GLAZE

1/2 cup (125 mL) icing (confectioner's) sugar

1/4 tsp (1 mL) almond extract

1 Tbsp (15 mL) milk, approximately

1 Tbsp (15 mL) chopped pecans (or walnuts or almonds), toasted (see p. 8), optional

WALNUT PIE WITH CRANBERRY CREAM

Serves 8

Tart pans are available at kitchen stores.

PIE CRUST

1 cup (250 mL) all-purpose flour

2 Tbsp (30 mL) granulated sugar

1/2 cup (125 mL) butter

1 large egg, fork-beaten

WALNUT FILLING

3 large eggs

1 cup (250 mL) golden corn syrup

1 cup (250 mL) brown sugar, packed

1/4 cup (60 mL) butter, melted

1 tsp (5 mL) vanilla extract

1/4 tsp (1 mL) ground cinnamon

1/4 tsp (1 mL) salt

2 cups (500 mL) walnuts, toasted (see p. 8) and coarsely chopped

(continued on next page)

Pie Crust: Place flour and sugar in a large bowl and rub in butter until mixture resembles coarse crumbs. Add egg and stir until a soft dough forms. Turn dough onto a lightly floured surface and knead very lightly just until dough is smooth. Roll pastry until large enough to fit into ungreased 10 inch (25 cm) tart pan. Place in tart pan and cover with plastic wrap. Place on baking sheet. Chill for 1 hour.

Preheat oven to 375°F (190°C). Line pastry with parchment paper. Fill halfway with dried beans or rice. Bake on bottom shelf of preheated oven for 15 minutes. Remove paper and beans. Cool pastry.

Walnut Filling: Whisk first 7 ingredients in a medium bowl until smooth. Stir in walnuts. Pour filling into cooled pastry shell; smooth top. Bake on bottom shelf of preheated oven for 35 to 40 minutes until firm. Filling may be a little wobbly in centre but will set on cooling. Place on a wire rack to cool. Serve pie warm or cold.

Cranberry Cream: Whip cream in a medium bowl until soft peaks form. Fold in remaining 3 ingredients. Serve with pie.

1 serving: 770 Calories; 48 g Total Fat (11 g Mono, 15 g Poly, 19 g Sat); 150 mg Cholesterol; 83 g Carbohydrate; 2 g Fibre; 9 g Protein; 290 mg Sodium

CRANBERRY CREAM

1 cup (250 mL) whipping cream

1/3 cup (75 mL) cranberry jelly, room temperature

1 to 2 Tbsp (15 to 30 mL) orange-flavoured liqueur (such as Cointreau)

1/4 tsp (1 mL) ground cinnamon

CHERRY PIE

Serves 8

This pie must be the easiest one in the world to make. The almond flavouring gives it a wonderful, unique taste. It is best served cold the day after it is prepared and is delicious with ice cream or custard.

PIE CRUST

1 cup (250 mL) all-purpose flour

3 Tbsp (45 mL) granulated sugar

1/2 cup (125 mL) butter, softened

FILLING

2 large eggs

1 cup (250 mL) granulated sugar

1/3 cup (75 mL) all-purpose flour

1 tsp (5 mL) almond extract

1/2 tsp (2 mL) baking powder

1/4 tsp (1 mL) salt

14 oz (398 mL) can pitted cherries, drained

icing sugar, for dusting (optional)

Pie Crust: Preheat oven to 325°F (160°C). Grease a 9 inch (23 cm) pie dish. Combine flour and sugar in a medium bowl. Rub in butter until well combined. Press pastry into bottom and up sides of prepared pie dish. Bake on bottom rack in preheated oven for 20 minutes.

Filling: Whisk first 6 ingredients in a medium bowl. Stir in cherries and pour into pastry shell (the pastry does not need to cool before adding the filling). Bake on bottom rack in preheated oven for 1 to 1 1/4 hours until pastry is browned and filling is set. Cool before covering and storing in refrigerator.

Dust with icing sugar before serving if desired.

1 serving: 330 Calories; 13 g Total Fat (3.5 g Mono, 0.5 g Poly, 8 g Sat); 65 mg Cholesterol; 52 g Carbohydrate; trace Fibre; 4 g Protein; 180 mg Sodium

Make-ahead Tip
The pie is best made a day ahead.

APPLE PIE WITH STREUSEL WALNUT TOPPING

Serves 8

This recipe is a slight twist on an old favourite, using a streusel mixture in place of a pastry top.

1 1/4 cups (300 mL) all-purpose flour

1/3 cup (75 mL) cold butter, chopped

1/4 cup (60 mL) icing (confectioner's) sugar

2 egg yolks (large)

1 Tbsp (15 mL) iced water, approximately

10 medium green apples, peeled, cored and coarsely chopped

1 cup (250 mL) granulated sugar

1/2 cup (125 mL) water

1/8 tsp (0.5 mL) salt

STREUSEL WALNUT TOPPING

1 cup (250 mL) all-purpose flour

2 tsp (10 mL) baking powder

1/2 cup (125 mL) cold butter, chopped

1 cup (250 mL) brown sugar, packed

1/2 cup (125 mL) walnuts, toasted (see p. 8) and chopped

Grease a 9 inch (23 cm) pie plate. Place flour in a large bowl and cut in butter until well combined; stir in sugar. Add egg yolks and enough iced water to mix to soft dough. Roll dough out on a lightly floured surface to 1/8 inch (3 mm) thickness. Place in prepared pie plate and trim and crimp edge. Cover with plastic wrap and refrigerate for 1 hour.

Preheat oven to 375°F (190°C). Combine apples, sugar, water and salt in a large saucepan. Bring to a boil then reduce heat to medium. Simmer, covered, for about 10 minutes, stirring occasionally, until apples are tender. Drain well and let cool.

Streusel Walnut Topping: Combine flour and baking powder in a medium bowl. Rub in butter until mixture resembles coarse crumbs. Stir in brown sugar and walnuts and stir until well combined. Spoon cooled apple mixture into pastry shell. Sprinkle with streusel walnut topping. Bake on bottom rack in preheated oven for about 50 minutes until base is browned. Cover loosely with foil during cooking if top is over-browning. Let stand for 15 minutes before cutting.

1 wedge: 660 Calories; 26 g Total Fat (6 g Mono, 4.5 g Poly, 13 g Sat); 105 mg Cholesterol; 107 g Carbohydrate; 4 g Fibre; 6 g Protein; 260 mg Sodium

Make-ahead Tip
The pie can be made a day ahead; serve cold. Or, have the pastry shell ready and in the pie plate, the apples cooked and topping ready a day ahead; store, covered, in the refrigerator. Remove from refrigerator 1 to 3 hours before assembling and baking. All you have to do is spoon apples into pastry, sprinkle with topping and bake.

BUTTER TARTS

Makes about 36

Make these tarts to give away during the festive season, or add them to a platter of sweets to serve family and friends.

2 x 9 oz (255 g) packages mini tart shells (2 inch, 5 cm, size)

2/3 cup (150 mL) dark raisins

2 tsp (10 mL) finely grated orange zest (see p. 8)

1/3 cup (75 mL) orange juice

1 3/4 cups (425 mL) brown sugar, packed

3/4 cup (175 mL) butter

1/4 cup (60 mL) whipping cream

2 tsp (10 mL) white vinegar

1 tsp (5 mL) vanilla extract

1/4 tsp (1 mL) salt

3 large eggs, fork-beaten

Preheat oven to 375°F (190°C). Place tart shells on 2 baking sheets.

Combine raisins, zest and juice in a small bowl. Let stand for 20 minutes.

Heat next 6 ingredients in a medium saucepan on medium. Stir until sugar dissolves; let cool. Add eggs and stir until well combined. Drain raisins and discard liquid. Divide raisins among tart shells. Spoon 2 tsp (10 mL) brown sugar mixture into each tart shell. Bake on bottom shelf of preheated oven for about 25 minutes until pastry is golden and filling is bubbling. Cool on baking sheets for 5 minutes before transferring to wire racks. Serve cold or warm.

1 tart: 160 Calories; 9 g Total Fat (3 g Mono, 1 g Poly, 4.5 g Sat); 25 mg Cholesterol; 20 g Carbohydrate; 0 g Fibre; trace Protein; 95 mg Sodium

PUMPKIN TART WITH A GINGER CRUST

Serves 8

This tart is best served cold.

8 oz (225 g) ginger cookies

1/3 cup (75 mL) pecans

1/2 cup (125 mL) butter, melted

FILLING

3 large eggs

1/3 cup (75 mL) brown sugar, packed

1/4 cup (60 mL) maple syrup

14 oz (398 mL) can pure pumpkin (no spices)

2/3 cup (150 mL) evaporated milk

1/2 tsp (2 mL) ground cinnamon

1/2 tsp (2 mL) ground ginger

1/4 tsp (1 mL) ground nutmeg

1/8 tsp (0.5 mL) salt

icing sugar, for dusting

Process cookies and pecans in a food processor until fine crumbs form. Combine butter and crumb mixture in a medium bowl. Using a flat-bottomed, straight-sided glass, press mixture into and up sides of ungreased 10 inch (25 cm) tart pan with removable base. Place on baking sheet. Chill for 30 minutes.

Filling: Preheat oven to 350°F (175°C). With an electric mixer, beat eggs, brown sugar and maple syrup in a large bowl until thick and pale.

Add next 6 ingredients and beat until well combined. Pour into prepared crust and smooth top. Bake in preheated oven for about 45 minutes until filling is set. Refrigerate for 6 hours or overnight before serving.

Dust with icing sugar just before serving if desired.

1 serving: 360 Calories; 20 g Total Fat (7 g Mono, 2 g Poly, 9 g Sat); 80 mg Cholesterol; 43 g Carbohydrate; 3 g Fibre; 6 g Protein; 350 mg Sodium

Make-ahead Tip
The tart is best made a day ahead; store in a sealed container in the refrigerator.

PANFORTE

Cuts into 32 wedges

This traditional Italian 'fruitcake' is best made a day or two before serving and is perfect after dinner with coffee. Cut into thin wedges, it makes a lovely gift—place wedges into cellophane bags or gift boxes and tie with a pretty ribbon.

1 cup (250 mL) all-purpose flour

1/3 cup (75 mL) cocoa powder

1/2 tsp (2 mL) ground cinnamon

1/2 tsp (2 mL) ground nutmeg

1/8 tsp (0.5 mL) salt

1 1/4 cups (300 mL) Brazil nuts, toasted and coarsely chopped

1 1/4 cups (300 mL) hazelnuts, toasted (see p. 8), peeled (see sidebar) and coarsely chopped

1 cup (250 mL) coarsely chopped dried figs

1 cup (250 mL) coarsely chopped glazed pineapple

1 cup (250 mL) coarsely chopped pitted dates

1/2 cup (125 mL) coarsely chopped dried apricots

2/3 cup (150 mL) granulated sugar

2/3 cup (150 mL) golden corn syrup

1/2 cup (125 mL) brown sugar, packed

1/4 cup (60 mL) water

7 oz (200 g) dark chocolate, melted (see p. 7)

Preheat oven to 325°F (160°C). Grease a 9 inch (23 cm) springform pan and line with 3 layers of parchment paper. Sift first 5 ingredients in a large bowl. Stir in next 6 ingredients.

Heat sugar, corn syrup, brown sugar and water in a small saucepan on medium until sugar is dissolved. Boil gently, uncovered, for 2 minutes, without stirring. Add to fruit and nut mixture and stir until well combined.

(continued on next page)

Add chocolate and stir until well combined. Press mixture firmly into prepared pan; this task is easier if you dampen your fingers with a little water first. Bake in preheated oven for 45 to 50 minutes until just firm. Let cool in pan completely before cutting into thin wedges.

※ *To peel toasted hazelnuts, wrap in a clean tea towel and rub vigorously. Most of the skin will peel away.*

1 wedge: 210 Calories; 9 g Total Fat (4 g Mono, 1.5 g Poly, 2.5 g Sat); 0 mg Cholesterol; 34 g Carbohydrate; 3 g Fibre; 3 g Protein; 20 mg Sodium.

Make-ahead Tip

The panforte can be made 1 week ahead; cover and store in a cool place.

CHOCOLATE TRUFFLES

Serves 6 to 8

It is best to use a good quality chocolate—it is easier to work with and the results are better.

LIME COCONUT TRUFFLES

1/4 cup (60 mL) whipping cream

1/4 cup (60 mL) butter

7 oz (200 g) white chocolate, chopped

2 Tbsp (30 mL) coconut-flavoured liqueur (such as Malibu)

1 Tbsp (15 mL) finely grated lime zest

7 oz (200 g) white chocolate, melted

1 1/4 cups medium unsweetened coconut, toasted (see p. 8)

CHERRY CHOCOLATE TRUFFLES

1/4 cup (60 mL) brandy

1/2 cup (125 mL) red glazed cherries, finely chopped

1/4 cup (60 mL) whipping cream

1/4 cup (60 mL) butter

7 oz (200 g) dark chocolate, chopped

7 oz (200 g) milk chocolate, melted (see p. 7)

chopped cherries, for garnishing

Lime Coconut Truffles (makes about 30): Stir whipping cream and butter in a small saucepan on medium-high until butter melts; remove from heat. Add chopped white chocolate and stir until melted.

Add liqueur and zest. Stir. Scrape mixture into a small bowl. Chill for 1 to 2 hours, stirring occasionally, until mixture is thick but not hard.

Drop rounded teaspoons of mixture onto a foil-lined baking sheet. Chill for about 1 hour until firm enough to roll into balls. Do not overchill. Roll into balls and place on same baking sheet; chill for 30 minutes. Dip each ball in melted white chocolate then roll in coconut, and place onto same baking sheet; chill until firm.

1 truffle: 120 Calories; 9 g Total Fat (0.5 g Mono, 0 g Poly, 6 g Sat); 10 mg Cholesterol; 9 g Carbohydrate; trace Fibre; trace Protein; 25 mg Sodium

Cherry Chocolate Truffles (makes about 35): Combine brandy and cherries in a small bowl and let stand for 15 minutes.

Stir whipping cream and butter in a small saucepan on medium-high until butter has melted; remove from heat. Add dark chocolate and stir until melted. Stir in cherry mixture. Scrape mixture into a small bowl. Chill for 1 to 2 hours, stirring occasionally, until mixture is thick but not hard.

(continued on next page)

Drop rounded teaspoons of mixture onto a foil-lined baking sheet. Chill for about 1 hour until firm enough to roll into balls. Do not overchill. Roll into balls and place on same baking sheet; chill for 30 minutes. Dip each ball in melted milk chocolate and place onto same baking sheet. Top with a piece of extra cherry before chocolate sets; chill.

1 truffle: 90 Calories; 5 g Total Fat (1.5 g Mono, 0 g Poly, 3 g Sat); 10 mg Cholesterol; 9 g Carbohydrate; trace Fibre; trace Protein; 15 mg Sodium

Make-ahead Tip

The truffles can be made a week ahead; keep in a sealed container in the refrigerator.

CASHEW AND APRICOT CHOCOLATE BARK

Makes about 30 pieces

For best results, use a good quality chocolate.

1 lb (454 g) milk chocolate, melted (see p. 7)

1 cup (250 mL) cashews, toasted (see p. 8), coarsely chopped

1/2 cup (125 mL) finely chopped dried apricots

1 Tbsp (15 mL) finely grated orange zest

Line a baking sheet with parchment paper. Combine all 4 ingredients in a large bowl. Spread thinly onto prepared baking sheet and let stand until cool. Refrigerate until firm. Break into 2 inch (5 cm) pieces.

1 piece: 120 Calories; 7 g Total Fat (2 g Mono, 0 g Poly, 2.5 g Sat); trace Cholesterol; 12 g Carbohydrate; 1 g Fibre; 2 g Protein; 15 mg Sodium

Make-ahead Tip
This recipe can be made a week ahead; store in a sealed container in refrigerator.

GINGER CHOCOLATE BISCOTTI

Makes about 24 pieces

This hard Italian-style biscuit is best served with coffee for dunking.

1 1/2 cups (375 mL) all-purpose flour

3 Tbsp (45 mL) cocoa powder

1/2 tsp (2 mL) baking powder

2/3 cup (150 mL) granulated sugar

1/4 cup (60 mL) butter, softened

2 large eggs

1/2 tsp (2 mL) vanilla extract

1/2 cup (125 mL) crystallized ginger, finely chopped

1 egg white (large), fork-beaten

2 tsp (10 mL) granulated sugar

Preheat oven to 350°F (175°C). Grease a baking sheet. Process first 4 ingredients in a food processor until mixed. Add butter and process until well combined. Add eggs and vanilla, and process until mixture forms a smooth dough.

Place dough on a lightly floured surface and knead in ginger. Divide dough into 2 equal portions and shape into logs about 8 inches (20 cm) long. Place diagonally, about 2 to 3 inches (5 to 7.5 cm) apart on prepared baking sheet. Brush with egg white, then sprinkle with second amount of sugar. Bake in preheated oven for about 30 minutes until firm and cracked across top. Let stand for 15 minutes before transferring to a cutting board. Reduce oven temperature to 325°F (160°C). Cut diagonally into 1/2 inch (12 mm) thick slices. Place each slice, cut-side up, on baking sheet. Bake for about 30 minutes until dry and crisp. Cool on wire racks.

1 piece: 100 Calories; 2.5 g Total Fat (0.5 g Mono, 0 g Poly, 1.5 g Sat); 15 mg Cholesterol; 17 g Carbohydrate; 0 g Fibre; 2 g Protein; 45 mg Sodium

GINGERBREAD MEN

Makes about 24 large cookies

Meringue powder can be found in kitchen specialty stores. Paste and powder food colourings will give a deeper, more intense colour than liquid colourings.

1 cup (250 mL) butter, softened

1 cup (250 mL) brown sugar, packed

1 large egg

1 cup (250 mL) fancy molasses

2 Tbsp (30 mL) milk

5 cups (1.25 L) all-purpose flour

1 1/2 tsp (7 mL) baking soda

1 Tbsp (15 mL) ground ginger

1 tsp (5 mL) ground cinnamon

1/4 tsp (1 mL) ground cloves

pinch of salt

ICING

1 cup (250 mL) icing sugar

3 Tbsp (45 mL) meringue powder

2 to 3 Tbsp (30 to 45 mL) water, approximately

red food colouring

brown food colouring

gold dragees (small edible candy beads), optional

Preheat oven to 350°F (175°C). Line cookie sheets with parchment paper. Beat butter and brown sugar in large bowl of a heavy-duty mixer until well combined and sugar is dissolved. Add egg, molasses and milk, and beat until well combined.

Sift next 6 ingredients into a large bowl. Add to butter mixture in 3 batches and beat until a smooth dough forms. Divide dough in half. Cover 1 portion with plastic wrap and set aside. Roll 1 portion onto a lightly floured surface until 1/4 inch (6 mm) thickness. Cut out shapes using 5 inch (12.5 cm) cookie cutter. Place gingerbread men 1 1/2 inches (4 cm) apart on prepared cookie sheets. Bake in preheated oven for about 15 minutes until just firm and starting to brown around edges. Let stand on cookie sheets for 10 minutes before transferring to wire racks to cool completely. Repeat with remaining dough. Off-cuts of uncooked dough can be re-rolled and cut out.

Icing: Place icing sugar and meringue powder in a small bowl and add enough water to make a fairly thick paste. Separate icing into 2 small bowls and colour one with red food colouring and other with brown colouring. Place each icing in 2 small piping bags fitted with a plain tip (see p. 7). Decorate gingerbread men as desired. Place dragees on icing, if desired, while still wet. Let stand for about 30 minutes until icing is set completely before storing.

1 cookie: 260 Calories; 8 g Total Fat (2 g Mono, 0 g Poly, 4.5 g Sat); 25 mg Cholesterol; 45 g Carbohydrate; trace Fibre; 3 g Protein; 160 mg Sodium

Make-ahead Tip

The gingerbread men can be made 1 week ahead; store in a sealed container in a cool, dry place.

CINNAMON SHORTBREAD

Makes 32 wedges

*This recipe is a shortbread pastry, so you may find some cracking
as you roll and shape the dough; just gently press any cracks together.
Omit the cinnamon for a plain shortbread.*

2 cups (500 mL) butter, softened
1 cup (250 mL) granulated sugar

4 cups (1 L) all-purpose flour
1 cup (250 mL) white rice flour
1 tsp (5 mL) ground cinnamon
(optional)
1/4 tsp (1 mL) salt

Preheat oven to 325°F (160°C). Grease 2 baking sheets.
Beat butter and sugar in a medium bowl with an electric
mixer until well combined.

Stir both flours, cinnamon and salt in a medium bowl. Add
to butter mixture in 3 batches, beating between each
addition until well combined. Turn onto a lightly floured
surface. Press together to form a soft dough. Divide
dough into 4 portions. Cover 3 portions with plastic
wrap and set aside. Roll 1 portion into a 7 inch (18 cm)
round disk. Carefully lift onto prepared baking sheet.
With a sharp knife, mark top into 8 even wedges and
prick all over with fork. Create a decorative edge by
pinching the pastry around the edge with lightly
floured fingers. Repeat with remaining dough. Place
two disks onto each baking sheet, about 1 to 2 inches
(2.5 to 5 cm) apart. Bake in preheated oven for about
30 minutes until very lightly golden. Let stand for
10 minutes before carefully transferring to wire racks
to cool.

*1 serving: 200 Calories; 12 g Total Fat (3 g Mono, 0 g Poly, 7 g Sat);
30 mg Cholesterol; 22 g Carbohydrate; trace Fibre; 2 g Protein;
100 mg Sodium*

RUM BALLS

Makes about 40

These treats can dry out quickly, so they are best eaten within 1 to 2 days of making.

8 oz (250 g) package vanilla-flavoured wafers

1 cup (250 mL) granulated sugar

1/4 cup (60 mL) golden corn syrup

1/2 cup (125 mL) spiced rum

7 oz (200 g) dark chocolate, chopped

1 1/2 cups (375 mL) chocolate sprinkles

Line a baking sheet with foil. Process wafers in food processor until mixture resembles fine crumbs.

Heat sugar, corn syrup and rum in a medium saucepan on medium-low, and stir until sugar dissolves; do not boil. Remove from heat. Add chocolate and stir until melted. Add wafer crumbs and stir until well combined. Drop 2 tsp (10 mL) mounds of mixture onto prepared baking sheets. Roll each mound into a ball, using lightly moistened hands. If mixture is not thick enough to roll, place in refrigerator for 5 to 10 minutes.

Place sprinkles on waxed paper or in shallow dish. Roll each ball into sprinkles while still moist. Place on same baking sheet and chill for about 1 hour until firm. Place into a sealed container and store in refrigerator. Remove from refrigerator about 1 hour before serving.

***1 rum ball:** 110 Calories; 4 g Total Fat (0.5 g Mono, 0 g Poly, 2 g Sat); 0 mg Cholesterol; 17 g Carbohydrate; trace Fibre; trace Protein; 35 mg Sodium*

Make-ahead Tip
The rum balls can be made 1 to 2 days ahead; store in a sealed container in refrigerator.

WHITE CHOCOLATE AND CRANBERRY COOKIES

Makes about 28

Fill your cookie jar with these yummy cookies or package them and give them away as gifts.

1 large egg

3/4 cup (175 mL) brown sugar, packed

1/4 cup (60 mL) granulated sugar

1/2 cup (125 mL) canola oil

1 tsp (5 mL) vanilla extract

1 cup (250 mL) all-purpose flour

1/2 tsp (2 mL) baking powder

1/4 tsp (1 mL) salt

8 oz (225 g) package white chocolate chips

3/4 cup (175 mL) dried cranberries

Line cookie sheets with parchment paper. Beat egg and both sugars in a small bowl with an electric mixer until pale and creamy. Add canola oil and vanilla and stir until combined. Sift flour, baking powder and salt into sugar mixture and stir.

Add chocolate and cranberries and mix well. Cover and refrigerate for 30 minutes.

Preheat oven to 350°F (175°C). Roll rounded tablespoons of mixture into balls. Place on prepared cookie sheets about 3 inches (7.5 cm) apart. Bake in preheated oven for about 12 minutes until golden. Let stand on cookie sheets for 5 minutes before transferring to wire rack to cool. Cool completely before storing.

1 cookie: 130 Calories; 6 g Total Fat (2.5 g Mono, 1 g Poly, 2.5 g Sat); trace Cholesterol; 18 g Carbohydrate; 0 g Fibre; trace Protein; 40 mg Sodium

SUGAR COOKIES

Makes about 48

Cut out and decorate cookies in any shapes and colours you desire.

3/4 cup (175 mL) butter, softened

1 cup (250 mL) granulated sugar

1/3 cup (75 mL) sour cream

1 large egg

1 tsp (5 mL) vanilla extract

2 3/4 cups (675 mL) all-purpose flour

1 tsp (5 mL) baking powder

1/4 tsp (1 mL) baking soda

1/4 tsp (1 mL) salt

1 egg white (large), fork-beaten

pink-coloured sugar

green-coloured sugar

ICING

1 cup (250 mL) icing sugar

3 Tbsp (45 mL) meringue powder

2 to 3 Tbsp (30 to 45 mL) water, approximately

green food colouring

red food colouring

silver dragees (small edible candy balls)

Line cookie sheets with parchment paper. Beat first 5 ingredients in a large bowl with an electric mixer until well combined and sugar is dissolved.

Combine next 4 ingredients in a medium bowl. Add to butter mixture in thirds. Beat until a soft dough forms. Turn dough onto lightly floured surface. Knead lightly until smooth. Divide dough in half. Wrap each half in plastic wrap and refrigerate for 30 minutes.

Preheat oven to 375°F (190°C). Roll dough on a lightly floured surface to 1/4 inch (6 mm) thickness. Cut out shapes using cutter of your choice lightly dipped in flour. Place on prepared cookie sheets about 1 inch (2.5 cm) apart. Brush half of cookies with egg white, then sprinkle with coloured sugar. Bake in preheated oven for about 8 minutes until edges of cookies are starting to lightly brown. Let stand on cookie sheets for 5 minutes before transferring to a wire rack to cool completely.

(continued on next page)

Icing: Place icing sugar and meringue powder in a small bowl and add enough water to mix to fairly thick paste. Place half of icing into another small bowl. Colour one icing pink and other green. Spoon each icing into piping bags fitted with plain small tips (see p. 7). Pipe icing onto undecorated cookies and decorate with dragees as desired. Let cookies stand until icing is set before storing.

1 cookie: *80 Calories; 3 g Total Fat (1 g Mono, 0 g Poly, 2 g Sat); 10 mg Cholesterol; 12 g Carbohydrate; 0 g Fibre; 1 g Protein; 50 mg Sodium*

Chocolate Peanut Butter Fudge

Makes 64 pieces

You can use crunchy or smooth peanut butter for this tasty treat.

1 cup (250 mL) small white marshmallows

2/3 cup (150 mL) peanut butter

1/2 cup (125 mL) butter

2 cups (500 mL) granulated sugar

1 cup (250 mL) sour cream

1/4 cup (60 mL) golden corn syrup

10 1/2 oz (300 g) dark chocolate, chopped

Grease an 8 x 8 inch (20 x 20 cm) baking pan and line with parchment paper. Heat marshmallows, peanut butter and butter in a small saucepan on medium for 3 to 4 minutes, stirring, until marshmallows and butter are melted.

Combine sugar, sour cream and corn syrup in a medium saucepan. Stir on medium-low until sugar is dissolved. Increase heat to high and bring to a boil, then immediately reduce heat to medium. Simmer, uncovered, stirring occasionally, until mixture reaches 220°F (110°C) on a candy thermometer. Mixture will turn a light caramel colour. Remove from heat and stir for 2 minutes.

(continued on next page)

Add peanut butter mixture and chocolate, and stir until melted. Immediately scrape into prepared pan; smooth top. Let stand until set. Refrigerate for about 3 hours until cold. Cut into 1 inch (2.5 cm) squares. Refrigerate fudge or keep in a cool, dry place.

1 piece: 90 Calories; 4.5 g Total Fat (0.5 g Mono, 0 g Poly, 2.5 g Sat); 5 mg Cholesterol; 11 g Carbohydrate; trace Fibre; trace Protein; 25 mg Sodium

Make-ahead Tip
This dessert can be made a week ahead; store in a sealed container in the refrigerator.

COCONUT NUT CLUSTERS

Makes about 30

*If you don't want to use foil liners or bon-bon cups, just drop
the mixture onto foil-lined baking sheets.*

**30 small foil or paper liners,
approximately**

**14 oz (400 g) white
chocolate, melted (see p. 7)**

**1 cup (250 mL) macadamia
nuts, toasted (see p. 8)
and coarsely chopped**

**1/2 cup (125 mL) shelled
pistachio nuts, toasted
(see p. 8)**

**1/2 cup (125 mL) medium
unsweetened coconut,
toasted (see p. 8)**

**melted dark chocolate, for
drizzling**

Place foil or paper liners on a baking sheet. Combine white
chocolate, macadamia nuts, pistachio nuts and coconut in
a small bowl. Drop 2 tsp (10 mL) mixture into each liner.
Refrigerate for about 3 hours until set.

Drizzle with melted chocolate.

*1 cluster: 120 Calories; 10 g Total Fat (3 g Mono, 0 g Poly, 4 g Sat); trace
Cholesterol; 10 g Carbohydrate; trace Fibre; 1 g Protein; 10 mg Sodium*

Make-ahead Tip
The clusters can be made a week ahead; store in a sealed
container in the refrigerator.

CHOCOLATE CARAMEL SQUARES

Makes about 32 squares or 64 triangles

Wrap these as gifts or serve with coffee for a decadent treat at the end of a meal.

COCONUT BASE

1 1/2 cups (375 mL)
all-purpose flour

1 1/2 cups (375 mL) medium
unsweetened coconut

1 1/4 cups (300 mL) brown
sugar, packed

3/4 cup (175 mL) butter,
melted

2 tsp (10 mL) baking
powder

1/8 tsp (0.5 mL) salt

CARAMEL FILLING

2 x 11 oz (300 mL) cans
sweetened condensed milk

3 Tbsp (45 mL) butter

3 Tbsp (45 mL) golden
corn syrup

1 tsp (5 mL) vanilla extract

CHOCOLATE TOPPING

7 oz (200 g) dark chocolate,
chopped

1/4 cup (60 mL) butter

Coconut Base: Preheat oven to 350°F (175°C). Grease a 9 x 13 inch (23 x 33 cm) baking pan and line with parchment paper, ensuring parchment paper comes 1 inch (2.5 cm) over long sides of pan. Combine all 6 ingredients in a large bowl. Press mixture into bottom of prepared pan. Bake in preheated oven for about 15 minutes until golden and brown around edges.

Caramel Filling: Stir all 4 ingredients in a medium saucepan on medium-low until butter melts. Stir constantly for about 10 minutes until mixture is slightly thickened, taking care not to burn mixture. Pour filling over hot coconut base and spread until smooth. Bake in preheated oven for about 10 minutes until bubbling and lightly brown around edges; cool.

Chocolate Topping: Stir chocolate and butter in a small saucepan on low for about 2 minutes until chocolate is almost melted. Remove from heat and stir until smooth. Spread warm topping over filling. Let stand at room temperature until cool. Cover and refrigerate for about 3 hours until cold. Holding edges of parchment paper, lift from pan. Cut into squares or triangles.

1 square: 240 Calories; 13 g Total Fat (2.5 g Mono, 0 g Poly, 9 g Sat); 25 mg Cholesterol; 30 g Carbohydrate; 1 g Fibre; 3 g Protein; 110 mg Sodium

Make-ahead Tip

These squares can be made 3 days ahead; store in a sealed container in the refrigerator. Let stand at room temperature for 30 minutes before serving.

HINT O' MINT SQUARES

Makes 36 squares

These Nanaimo bar–type squares have a festive green layer and a great minty-chocolate flavour.

1 cup (250 mL) icing (confectioner's) sugar

1/4 cup (60 mL) butter (or hard margarine), softened

1/2 tsp (2 mL) peppermint extract

2 drops green food colouring

1/2 cup (125 mL) butter (or hard margarine)

1/4 cup (60 mL) cocoa, sifted if lumpy

1/4 cup (60 mL) granulated sugar

1 large egg, fork-beaten

3/4 cup (175 mL) chocolate wafer crumbs

3/4 cup (175 mL) flaked coconut

3/4 cup (175 mL) graham cracker crumbs

3/4 cup (175 mL) semi-sweet chocolate chips

2 1/2 Tbsp (37 mL) butter (or hard margarine), melted

Beat icing sugar, first amount of butter, extract and food colouring in a small bowl until smooth. Press firmly in a waxed paper–lined 9 x 9 inch (23 x 23 cm) pan. Freeze until firm.

Combine second amount of butter, cocoa and sugar in large saucepan on medium. Heat and stir until sugar is dissolved. Remove from heat. Quickly whisk in egg until thickened slightly.

Add wafer crumbs, coconut and cracker crumbs. Stir well. Scatter half of crumb mixture into a separate foil-lined 9 x 9 inch (23 x 23 cm) pan. Remove frozen peppermint layer from pan. Turn upside down over crumb mixture. Peel off waxed paper. Scatter remaining half of crumb mixture over peppermint layer. Pack firmly into pan.

Heat chocolate chips and third amount of butter in a small heavy saucepan on lowest heat, stirring often, until chocolate is almost melted. Do not overheat. Stir until smooth. Pour over squares. Spread evenly. Let stand until chocolate is firm.

1 square: 104 Calories; 6.8 g Total Fat (1.8 g Mono, 0.4 g Poly, 4.2 g Sat); 17 mg Cholesterol; 11 g Carbohydrate; 1 g Fibre; 1 g Protein; 63 mg Sodium

ICEBOX RIBBONS

Makes about 66

*A pretty, three-layered cookie. Freezes well before, or after, baking.
Choose your favourite type of nuts.*

1 cup (250 mL) butter (or hard margarine), softened	Beat butter and sugar in a large bowl. Add egg and vanilla. Beat well.
1 cup (250 mL) granulated sugar	
1 large egg	
1 tsp (5 mL) vanilla extract	

1 cup (250 mL) butter (or
hard margarine), softened

1 cup (250 mL) granulated
sugar

1 large egg

1 tsp (5 mL) vanilla extract

2 1/2 cups (625 mL)
all-purpose flour

1 tsp (5 mL) baking powder

1/4 tsp (1 mL) salt

red liquid (or paste) food
colouring

1/4 cup (60 mL) chopped
red glazed cherries

1/3 cup (75 mL) medium
unsweetened coconut

1/3 cup (75 mL) semi-sweet
chocolate chips

1/3 cup (75 mL) chopped
nuts

Beat butter and sugar in a large bowl. Add egg and vanilla. Beat well.

Combine flour, baking powder and salt in a medium bowl. Add to butter mixture. Stir until stiff dough forms. Divide dough into 3 equal portions.

Knead enough red food colouring into 1 portion of dough until pink. Add cherries. Knead until evenly distributed. Press in foil-lined 8 x 4 x 3 inch (20 x 10 x 7.5 cm) loaf pan.

Add coconut to second portion of dough. Knead until evenly distributed. Press evenly over pink layer.

Heat chocolate chips in small heavy saucepan on low, stirring often, until almost melted. Do not overheat. Remove from heat. Stir until smooth. Add chocolate and nuts to third portion of dough. Knead until no streaks remain. Press evenly over coconut layer. Cover with plastic wrap. Chill overnight. Remove from pan. Remove and discard foil. Cut into 1/4 inch (6 mm) thick slices. Cut each slice into 3 pieces. Arrange slices, about 2 inches (5 cm) apart, on greased cookie sheets. Bake in 350°F (175°C) oven for 10 to 12 minutes until edges are golden. Let stand on cookie sheets for 5 minutes before removing to wire racks to cool.

1 cookie: 72 Calories; 4 g Total Fat (2.1 g Mono, 0.6 g Poly, 1.1 g Sat); 3 mg Cholesterol; 8 g Carbohydrate; trace Fibre; 1 g Protein; 50 mg Sodium

HOLIDAY COFFEE AND TEA

Each recipe serves 4

Whether your guests favour coffee or tea, you'll be able to offer them the perfect after-dinner drinks—a dark, fragrant coffee or a comforting, apple pie–scented tea.

ALMOND COFFEE

4 cups (1 L) hot strong prepared coffee (or espresso)

1/2 cup (125 mL) almond-flavoured liqueur (such as Amaretto) or almond-flavoured syrup (such as Torani's)

1/4 cup (60 mL) half-and-half cream (or milk)

4 tsp (20 mL) brown sugar, packed

1/2 cup (125 mL) whipped cream (or frozen whipped topping, thawed)

2 Tbsp (30 mL) sliced almonds, toasted (see p. 8)

sprinkle of cocoa, sifted if lumpy

(continued on next page)

Almond Coffee: Combine first 4 ingredients in an 8 cup (2 L) liquid measure or small heatproof pitcher. Pour into 4 large mugs.

Top each with whipped cream. Sprinkle almonds and cocoa over top.

1 serving: 210 Calories; 13 g Total Fat (4.5 g Mono, 1 g Poly, 7 g Sat); 40 mg Cholesterol; 15 g Carbohydrate; 0 g Fibre; 2 g Protein; 25 mg Sodium

Caramel Apple Cider: Heat first 4 ingredients in a large saucepan until boiling. Remove from heat. Add tea bag. Cover. Let steep for 5 minutes. Remove and discard tea bag and cinnamon stick. Ladle into 4 large mugs.

Top each with about 1/3 cup (75 mL) whipped cream. Put ice cream topping into small resealable freezer bag. Cut tiny hole in 1 corner. Squeeze over whipped cream in zigzag pattern. Dust cinnamon over top. Add 1 cinnamon stick to each mug.

1 serving: 410 Calories; 26 g Total Fat (7 g Mono, 1 g Poly, 16 g Sat); 90 mg Cholesterol; 48 g Carbohydrate; 0 g Fibre; 2 g Protein; 90 mg Sodium

CARAMEL APPLE CIDER

4 cups (1 L) apple juice (or cider)

2 cups (500 mL) water

2 Tbsp (30 mL) brown sugar, packed

1 cinnamon stick (4 inch, 10 cm, length)

1 orange pekoe tea bag

1 1/3 cups (325 mL) whipped cream (or prepared dessert topping)

3 Tbsp (45 mL) thick caramel ice cream topping

sprinkle of ground cinnamon (optional)

4 cinnamon sticks (4 inch, 10 cm, length), optional

CRANBERRY WARMER

Serves 10

8 cups (2 L) cranberry juice

4 cups (1 L) pear (or apple) juice

3 medium pears, peeled and chopped

2/3 cup (150 mL) small cranberries

2 x 5 inch (12.5 cm) pieces orange peel

2 cinnamon sticks

10 whole cloves

Combine all 7 ingredients in a slow cooker. Heat, covered, on Low for 8 to 10 hours or on High for 4 to 5 hours. Remove peel, cinnamon sticks and cloves before serving.

1 serving: 180 Calories; 0 g Total Fat (0 g Mono, 0 g Poly, 0 g Sat); 0 mg Cholesterol; 46 g Carbohydrate; 2 g Fibre; 0 g Protein; 25 mg Sodium

HOT CHOCOLATE

Serves 4

3 cups (750 mL) milk

1/2 cup (125 mL) half-and-half cream

10 1/2 oz (300 g) dark chocolate, chopped

1/4 tsp (1 mL) ground cinnamon

3/4 cup (175 mL) coffee-flavoured liqueur (such as Kahlúa), optional

1 cup (250 mL) whipping cream

instant hot chocolate mix, for garnish

Heat milk and cream in a medium saucepan on medium-high until bubbling. Remove from heat and add chocolate; stir until melted. Add cinnamon and liqueur, and stir until well combined. Heat mixture on medium until hot but not boiling. Beat whipping cream with an electric mixer until soft peaks form. Pour hot chocolate into warmed cups, top with whipped cream and sprinkle with chocolate mix.

1 serving: 790 Calories; 49 g Total Fat (7 g Mono, 0.5 g Poly, 29 g Sat); 100 mg Cholesterol; 70 g Carbohydrate; 6 g Fibre; 14 g Protein; 150 mg Sodium

MULLED WINE

Serves 6

2 x 750 mL bottles pinot noir or merlot

1 cup (250 mL) port

1/2 cup (125 mL) crystallized ginger, chopped

2 cinnamon sticks

6 whole cloves

5 cardamom pods, bruised (see p. 6)

1 medium orange, sliced

2/3 cup (150 mL) brown sugar, packed

Combine all 8 ingredients in a slow cooker. Heat, covered, on Low for 8 to 10 hours or on High for 4 to 5 hours. Remove cinnamon sticks, cloves and cardamom pods before serving. Keep warm.

1 serving: 450 Calories; 0 g Total Fat (0 g Mono, 0 g Poly, 0 g Sat); 0 mg Cholesterol; 56 g Carbohydrate; trace Fibre; 0 g Protein; 35 mg Sodium

PINEAPPLE AND STRAWBERRY COCKTAIL

Serves 4

2 cups (500 mL) pineapple juice

1/2 cup (125 mL) vodka

1/2 cup (125 mL) orange-flavoured liqueur
(such as Cointreau)

2 cups (500 mL) frozen strawberries

1 Tbsp (15 mL) lime juice

Process all 5 ingredients in a blender until
smooth.

1 serving: 210 *Calories; 0 g Total Fat
(0 g Mono, 0 g Poly, 0 g Sat); 0 mg Cholesterol;
28 g Carbohydrate; 2 g Fibre; trace Protein;
0 mg Sodium*

EGGNOG

Serves 4

6 egg yolks

1/2 cup (125 mL) granulated sugar

2 cups (500 mL) half-and-half cream

1/2 tsp (2 mL) ground nutmeg

1/8 tsp (0.5 mL) ground cinnamon

2/3 cup (150 mL) spiced rum

ground nutmeg, for sprinkling (optional)

Whisk yolks and sugar in medium bowl until
sugar dissolves. Heat cream in a medium
saucepan until bubbles appear around
side of pan. Gradually whisk hot cream
into egg mixture. Pour mixture back into
saucepan and add nutmeg and cinnamon.
Stir constantly on medium-low until mixture
coats the back of a spoon. Remove from heat
and stir in rum. Sprinkle individual servings
with extra nutmeg if desired.

*1 serving: 420 Calories; 21 g Total Fat (7 g Mono,
1.5 g Poly, 11 g Sat); 300 mg Cholesterol;
31 g Carbohydrate; 0 g Fibre; 8 g Protein;
60 mg Sodium*

PEACH LIME DAIQUIRIS

Serves 2

12 1/2 oz (398 mL) can peaches
with light syrup

1/2 cup (125 mL) white rum

1/3 cup (75 mL) orange-flavoured liqueur
(such as Cointreau)

1/2 cup (125 mL) lime juice

1 cup (250 mL) ice cubes

Place all 5 ingredients in a blender and
process until smooth.

*1 serving: 350 Calories; 0 g Total Fat (0 g Mono,
0 g Poly, 0 g Sat); 0 mg Cholesterol;
47 g Carbohydrate; 3 g Fibre; 1 g Protein,
10 mg Sodium*

INDEX